Isaac Newton's Scalder, Abraham, Prophesies the End of the World, & Other Poems

Carlo Parcelli

DEDICATED TO
Liam Rector & Larry Fox

CONTENTS

Carlo Parcelli

Part I: Isaac Newton's Scalder, Abraham, Prophesies the End of the World

*Definition: Scalder – the servant who plucked feathers from fowl
and the hair and bristles from pigs, goats, sheep etc. using
scalding water.*

The moon be a trencher for all I know,
    Pocked a poor castin' and in need of a good scrub.
I be, Abraham, Master Isaac's scalder,
    What sweat the bristle out a hog
      Or weep a fat goose's down.
  Me master most frets about the Second Comin';
    This creation's end and riddance
What be ta him and all
    But a callin' ta one better,
  And sings praises even as he hastens,
    Ta my mind, Earth ta kingdom come.
For what be worse, those what hope and pray
    For the world's end,
  And for their righteous salvation
Or those what forsake kith and kin,
    And, what by their arts, shape that end.
    What in Sir Isaac flows bofe,
Is what me, his servant see, what he call oaf.
    So might it be better
  Me master not be a mathematicus,
Or course his base metals a'lead and sulphur
  What foul the estate and make me toddles sick.
  For it be London plague what brings him here
    Among us poor but quick.
And don' he go on about the true estate
  A'Daniel and John a Revelation or ta denoue
What sort be ta his mind

Forbodes fallacious speculation.
What Sir Isaac curse this bloke Cerinthus
    What accounts that after the Second Comin',
  Jerusalem for a millennium bask in carnal rites.
Say I, Master might we not be prudent and consider such
    What I not mind showin' a bit a'me third leg
Ta some winsome sally up some holy scullery,
    Be it Jesus own estate ta sanctify.
Ta what he rail and threat me with dispatch,
  Me what be labored wif a trough ta hew
    And a roof ta thatch.
What Sir Isaac frough signs and scripture
  And the like, work day and night ta
    Put our end at 2060 annus domini.
So certain, the roof need a proper patch,
  Or our deaf ta catch, or have our froats cut
For lack of a lock and proper latch and
  Meet a salvation as bereft as his bodily mettle be.
    And those a that time certain be so ordained
  For me master be privy ta all things, so he tells me.
Sir Isaac be satiate a mind, but a body he be a pauper.
    He eats naught what the cooks prepare
And loiters down the sheds famished ta counsel
    Us yeomen about his goblin - gravity and his calculus
  And what this German Leibniz pilfered his thoughts
    What he say these bloody krauts naught be trusted.
And there be some fancy about a cannonball
    What wheel about the earf or such
But unlike the stars the missiles never fall;
    Or these engines what blaspheme
  Flesh and soul wif their ragin' infernos
    What dim me dreams a' 'carnal pleasures'
    And in me frights detach the arms and legs
    A'me and me little mites.
Did not good Mr. Milton put in Satan's maw,
  The words "To wage by force or guile eternal warre"?
Be, by blood a'Christ, me imperial Master's
    Very evangelizin' call.
  And what this Italian, Bruno,

What be dear ta Sidney and Dee
Portend in his book what be called
   La Cena de le Ceneri, Or Ash Wednesday Supper,
What, like cattle, hereabouts
  We chattle dine a'ashcake and water.
     What evils such imperious impose
Cite I from Sir Isaac's very larder a'books
    What me master be out and about
  Discursin' some hell-bent folly,
      Ere I transpose what the Nolan indict
        And give Raleigh's world the lie;
What be utter germane ta our woeful plight
    For this good sir, Bruno, write:
  "The helmsmen of explorations schemes
How to vex the tranquility a'uvvers;
    To profane their guardian spirits;
To mix what our prudent Muvver Nature deny;
    To redouble men's lust for dealin's and
To add to the vices of one people those of anuvver
  To breed new follies wif cannon and mailed fist
 And set up unheard lunacies
     Where none before exist,"
And wif bloody dispatch they allot a just god and
  With glint a'forged incisors,
    "Claim the stronger be the wiser."
What the gentry even fashion a weapon a sagacity.
  Ta take god's wit and forge a fang a'it.
What an ox be a dumb beast, but of service,
  What the fox be more akin ta me master's purpose.
What Bruno on Ash Wednesday out the true nature
   A'the philosopher's stone wif the likes
 A'the Cabots, Drake, Hawkins and Raleigh,
Men what for earfly fortune
    Sear a cross upon the sea:
  "Showin' men new ways, instruments,
And arts what ta master
    And slaughter one anuvver.
But don't doubt there be a time ta come,
   Havin' licked their wounds,

Those what chafe a'their chains
            Will oblige retribution,
        Composed a'similar torments or worse,
    A recompense what be none uvver than
            The very pernicious inventions and vain intents
                What be now the helmsmens' curse."
What me master's creations not only auger an end time
            But urge on its circumstance.
He what by his diabolicals and wanton study a uvvers' evil
            Hasten that day what John a'Patmos ordain,
When this muddle a'who be righteous and who naught,
    A day what sort boundless glory from eternal pain.
And what wif me bed above his lab'ratory
        I gets me headaches, nightmares,
            Torment and predilections
    A such ill-borne, murderous nature
        What the church hang me
            Wif no guilt put upon the source
Such be me Master's standin',
        Wif his rooms at Cambridge
    And now here at the Thorpe.
But I know, I do, what be his tenet
        Upon the Trinity.
    What me pluckin' pheasants and
Seein' clear as Paul on the road ta Damascus.
    What wif me night sweats
Doth the Bible be but the prophecy
        A'the Heavens and the stars,
Naught but the revel a'Bruno and Dee.
  For Saul be Paul a'the Almighty's alchemy,
What read therein the Apocalypse
            And the Second Comin'.
    And precise Sir Isaac forecast
    Such appall beset mankind in 2060.
        What Jesus be our hourglass
        And me master be its instrument,
What all this measure and experiment
  Be but the engines a'the final denouement.
        What be a principle a'his larder a'books,

If not his own endeavors
    What there be a bit a'demiurge in these Taccolas and
Da Vincis, what not abashed ta look upon a naked god;
    Yet blanch a'the petty wrath a'ignorant bishops,
    What leaves but me to honor his trust,
By what I mean bofe god and Sir Isaac,
        Lest by some authority I be bound over.
These what would tear apart the very flesh
    What current much gives me pleasure.
        If it be simple to know thus,
Be I simple before god and the devil
        And concourse wif mortal nature
Having pleased me mortal meat in due time.
    But to force god's word on a world
        What abides anuvver?
Better such aggrieves be strangled in the crib,
    And the many a'days I feel ta starve here
        Than ta sup me rightful board.
Be there trufe in Daniel or John but ciphers
    A'star crossed mutterin' what me Master
        Doth claim ta depise.
What sensible Bruno embrace and teachin's
        He would wish to impart ta Dee's circle
    If not he be carried to the stake,
        What I cross meself and
    Praise present times not warrant me offenses,
    What sign be license ta speak of an end
        And foster no further determination.
What be derived from caution and grammar
    Where tense say a fact be modal
        And time be not place but consequent,
        As Heraclitus confer.
Me, I think we ought not contract
    Wif the stars nor wif our beakers and mortars.
What I trust me loins and that abide behind
        The scullery wif some fine filly
Rather than anuvver learned cohesion
        At the whipping tongue a'Sir Isaac
As he makes the Second Comin' man's handiwork.

An 'apocalyptic pleonasm' is what Mr. Pepys
Named it on which I once dared discourse
        Whilst groomin' his horse.
Only time I saw me Sir Isaac smile though in discord.
    "My work, a cosmic 'fait accompli?" he said.
Then a pained grin and a hard scowl,
        'Bout dislodged a'me bowel.
    "Always wif your arcadian logic, eh Abraham.
A fine scalder, Mr. Pepys, and a tolerable butcher too.
   Talks too much as these bumpkins are wont to do."
    What that night in me dreams
I see a poly-eyed obelisk,
        And a desert lit wif brimstone
    Like the earf disgorged the sun.
And it be hard pressed against our flesh
        What blew off bone in a bloody mist.
So I asked meself what be this?
    Better to sleep in the barn
  Than to suffer this Devil's scorn,
        Or even press me service else,
For who better than me to judge me fate
    Above what be a demon's number
        And alchemical advocate.
What me Master say I be non uvver than his Daniel
    But if be so, he be no Nebuchadnezzar
        What forget his dream,
What be portent a'me phantasms and seizures?
    What fumes a'his boiling beakers rise
        Like souls withering up from their graves,
What trouble me days wif these ravings.
    Why be I so cursed a'such a master?!
Why this burden be upon me,
            What me tether be but humble work?
        Certain I not worthy a'Gethsemane.
God, you make the laws and all your prophets
    Get free range ta test the likes a'me.
But I'd sooner garrote the bastards
    Than suffer such in the name a'thee.
They be forlorn and drive all things into lunacy.

And what be worse be the godly indifference
Me Master show toward us patchy humanity.
          We know there be best ta aspire ta be better.
     But Sir Isaac know not what specimen he be,
His virginity what be naught a'just a woman
          But a grandiose tendering ta the world.
     His inchoate rages, suspicious of us mere clods
What but labor at what be our wages duty.
          A grotesque a occult arts, numbers and base alchemy
               And all the poisons such impart,
          What will certain raze the world
               If they find common industry.
     Warden of the Mint be measure a'his alchemy.
          He what be some alien stain.
                    Some dark angel flung down by Thee
          To end us all. Though me hopes
               Not before me soul departs,
     Frough creations harmonious spagyrical arts,
And the earf takes back the bits what Nature rots.
          Does not Ovid report
Zeus mint a cow a poor Io,
          Or knobby swan a'hisself?
And dun't the bible attest Jesus
          Sweat wine a'water?
What we yeoman do
          Appreciate a bit a'alchemy,
     So we poach an alembic or two,
Ta craft a still what, like our Lord,
          Our spirits ta lift and purify.
     Anointed thus wif holy water
          What we call red ribbon,
We heat and cool our Noah's wine,
     Below the hangin' draft horse halters
Wif a care worn work bench be our altar.
     What we brew aqua vitae,
          Or what be brandy ta our betters.
And what the Porter get drunk as a blood
     And smash a beaker on the rim of a tub,
          What the master be a bloody prick

And beat the man for want of an alembic
What be blown in Grantham for a pence
  Or for but a farthing or better,
     We contract a copper still.
What our master thump the bloke
   Wif the knob a'his cane many a stroke,
    And split his pate.
Our docile minds must be sotted
   What ta occasion such consequence
    From our betters,
 And, aye, we be full grown blokes,
   At the cudgel end of a stick.
But a master's omits be praised as far sighted,
  What he bring about all creation's demise,
    What like frogs in the kettle,
   Whivver we all, boil to the quick.
Does it not seem we appall him by our existence?
   That his calculus be a design ta end us all,
What there be born as I speak
  Future demigods what have the cheek
    Ta heed his call.
  Even, as I stand before the Shire's stall
  Now I see their engines stomp and steam
Beyond the commons and know not
    If I swoon or dream.
   Such be the vapors what suss me room,
 And I fall sick a'earf and cleaved a kingdom come.
What he be a plague wif'in a plague
   What return to his estate wif his fitful temper.
   And for all their beneficence,
Sir Isaac's inventions bend toward darkness
  Even as he bent god's light wif his water stone.
 But where Mr. Locke be far too demure,
Mr. Pepys, he be randy sure
  What ta embroil me master wif ready wenches.
But not him though his manner be grand
  His stench be a'stale sweat and ass,
What we dig a new privy well down wind
  Our Sir Isaac, workin' away, prefer ta soil hisself,

What offend both sense and senses,
He not abate a reckoning or leave off a task,
　　Since ta me master the alchemical arts,
Jugglin' sums and the bible be all what quenches.
　And so many acrid vapors course his nose,
A prominent appendage, I might add,
　　　What now no odor impose.
What he impart his wrath upon poor Locke,
　No doubt, misplacing blame
For the art of passion Mr. Pepys proposed.
　　　Or rant the night frough 'bout
　　Some blow from Leibniz what Clarke relate
By minds what dwarf our common desires
　　　To eat and procreate,
What confound the court itself and
　　Keep all the scholars and sages in deep debate.
　　　What besides his calculus and
Constant labors he undertook,
　Sir Isaac have but three tribulations;
The plague, the Great Fire, and Mr. Robert Hooke.
　　The teef a'Descartes' gears may be greased
For the celestial wrench a'me Master's pull.
　　But before Sir Isaac, vile Hooke cut new gears,
Out a'nowhere, at right angles what divine
　　What they call the inverse law and
Brings me master ta rage and salty tears?
　　Me master say light be
　　　But parts like bits or grains.
What that knave, Hooke,
　Writ light be shaped a'waves and bends,
　　And all manner a'wild apothegms.
　　And what be I but
What Sir Isaac name a wanton oaf
　Care not if be curves or crumbs or prove be bofe.
　　These claim close be the harmonies a'nature
　What spur but row and quarrel?
I weary a'suffering me master's wrath
　What Mr. Hooke accomplish wif his distant acts.
What these bloody enlightened blokes know

A'the celestial accords,
What be a cynical temperament and caustic tongue;
    Cantankerous, envious, vengeful for vain rewards,
  What in neiver their own reckoning
      Nor by assay can do no wrong.
What spur me master in hot hate
      Ta place Mr. Hooke's portrait among the hogs
  What nuzzle and prate upon it in the muck.
Don' I say Sir Isaac's malady denies prudent Nature,
    The occasional shag, what lack thereof
        Chrism in us bloods some mental depravity.
Or me Masters lead, mercury, arsenic and such
        What linger in our water and air,
    In his pursuit a'gold be poisons
            What rot our guts like a true Republic,
  Rich, poor, man, woman or child, young and old
        Sickened by the exhaust a'his pursuit a'gold
As we expire by dint a'the very blackness
        That allays our cold.
      And be it so, Warden a'the Mint
    Be the measure a'me master's alchemy;
He conjure poisons what by their nature ta wares
        Find favor wif Britain's manufactory,
What they be bound ta every port
        Ta confound the matter a'Bruno's discord.
May one a'Sir Isaac's comets come like a gryphon's tail
  And sweep me master to his judgement,
So conspicuous be our lord ta rant and rail
      Against any creature what not be in accord
          Wif his counts and considerations.
Better he run his contrives and cons
    On the bloody Trinity dons
What ta stamp and steam on the family farm
    Like some broodmare put to pasture.
What the man's tongue be a lash
      His humours inconstant and his judgments rash.
Master a'the universe and conquistador a'thatch.
  What methinks, Sir Isaac, the bloody sorcerer,
    Sooner raise the dead than raise a barn;

Or raze all that went before;
Sans balls, sans pity, sans humor and sans charm.
　　What this John Keill were ta never defend me master
Ta raise such alarums in Sir Isaac's mind
　　What spell disaster for us common folk.
What be about our daily employ under our master's yolk;
　　What be desperate minions sick of our indenture
And fear we be but precurse for the world.
Me thinks he possess his own premise and surmise
　　About his mafematical apocalypse
When the earth will shake and the dead will rise.
　　　Ta me mind it's his intent what be in doubt.
　　What does he despise his species to such a degree
That the willful bedlamite
　　Bring about all living creature's expiry?
　　Ends and means he calculate
Wif his John a'Patmos and Daniel's Book.
　　But gives not us yeomen a second look.
I know he not love me,
　　　And ain't I one a'god's own.
Me be no ragman, nay, a'mere skin and bone.
　　I picks his quills and renders his tallow.
And when Apollo quit him, constellate him
　　Wif candles, a light more than the heavens,
　　Ta quell the night and his studies allow
　　　Such that his labors can follow.
　　What at me leanest jape he sends me ta hell?
For us mortals need merriment
　　Ta grapple wif our heres and nows.
　What his eye sees and ear hears
　　Our joy and pleasures our guffaws and howls
As eternal war between heaven and hell no doubt.
But us poor benighted know, he be no scented angel,
　　What not much bathe and,
　　　Knighted or no, Sir Isaac's fumes be infernal.
And his rank smell assist his prudery,
　　For no fair dell or spry widow venture near.
　Me master surpass Enoch's stink
　　　What wooze god's very angels

What in a chariot and horses charred in flames
   The prophet like a fiery barb passed ta heaven.
Sir Isaac glowed ruddy as an oven
      What me and Paget
    Turn his tube upon the coven a'nuns
Bathin' nude in the river Witham,
     The ones what convent be adjoined
   The Papist chapel not more than half a mile.
Oh be I fabulous Acteon, ta behold such lewd sights
     As though they be close upon me!
What our master trespass the heavens
      As we do these popish cunts,
    What nigh vision rent me wif lust.
And Artemis brand me a stag
      While me master be but a protestant.
   What priest and they be little more than fiends
  What deny the crown, god's good authority.
For we but look on demons, I tells him,
    That our souls be better informed
     What the devil pose his alarum
And tempt us unbeknownst
    As these Catholic bawds be god's good women,
What we capture close wif his magic tube,
   Gay as an inquisitor's flame, splashin' and swimmin'.
But Sir Isaac abash me and Paget wif our pranks,
    What we torment Our Lord's righteous soul
  "Indulgin' in the lust a defilin' passion," what he cite
     Priggish as Paul, the shite
What blindly buggers all mankind
    For ardor a'his goal.
But me master though be horned true, is no watcher
     What he be estranged a'women folk.
While fallen though they be,
    The 'watchers' be randy blokes
   What take human wives and
  Teach men the use a'arms and false astrology,
And tutor in the movement a'the clouds
   No earth bound pupil seem attend,
    For such science still fail prophecy.

Or Enoch's 'watchers' what teach the signs
     A the sun and the moon
As though they be posted on Great Norf Road.
    Or this winged astrologer Kokobiel
        What conveniently have exact
   A thousand pranksters for each day a'the solar year.
But fear not, Sir Isaac, I not be one.
    Nor borne by any bosh a'your good book.
Me eyes spy your glass. Flesh fire me prick.
     So I urged on by me lusts have a look.
There be no devil in it, namore than happenstance.
     What me prospect be a naked nun
    And hopes of a furious jiggery
Wif a heretics want of an Anglican prick,
    I spies me happy chance.
What I behold from a woman's hips
     If traced by the eye wif a stick on a string,
  Like Mercury the orbit doth form an ellipse.
     Our judgements be enough clouded,
For our inventions be but mortal expressions.
    And it be the odd day, indeed,
What me grunting exuberance
      Put your inverse law upon display,
What some future swell from Oxford or Cambridge
     Wif a mind like a fiery furnace,
  Its light bending the rosy cleat,
     Will no doubt toss away.
What Sir Isaac flee the London plague
   Wif his satchel and leggin's all ridden wif such -
     Fleas I mean, what me master's prick
Safeguarded by its stench be assured,
    His organ tarry pure a'heart,
  What his pokin' about his fumes and vapors
Has ceded smell from his sense's lexicon.
   What Master Crosspatch attend
      Upon his exile from London town
And see burgeoning stocks a'pen and sty,
    Such a raft a'pork and mutton,
    And so many geese and ducks,

And sacks a'down,
What we yeomen tend and so multiply.
And he orders we sell the surplus
At Grantham market where the numbers swell
East Enders in flight a'the plague as well.
And so it seems let the devil do his best
And take many a soul, crones, babes and all.
Still our numbers be never at rest,
And business be brisk at our stall.
But whatever the congress a'rats and fleas
Sir Isaac's fluxes and analyticals will bring
All creation to its knees.
None fear fleeing mere London
To mend upon the country air
But decamp ta distant orbs
What Sir Isaac's tube doth make aware.
Other worlds what be the Nolan's touch,
And me Master's tallies ta take them there.
And good riddance I say,
Just spare me food, drink and cunny,
And thank ya very much.
And by such spare us the bible's fate
And pray by dint a'Sir Isaac's wit
It not be too late.
For the plague make plain for all wif eyes
What Johnny Patmos claims a'the resurrect,
By Sir Isaac's reckonings, though given his
Simple faif, seems but utterly circumspect.
Now no mortal man care rise again
But when those diabolical few do
Will by succor extinguish not the quiddity
But merely the agent a'the pain,
What sharper stick be than its phantom.
What the Midas touch be in any form,
From fancies spread a gold like a plague
Ta be so forlorn and bereft
As ta rape thy swaddlin' mother
And then take flight but ta ravage another.
What more ta disturb celestial peace

By spinning flesh and bone across the heavens,
   When it be your cupidity what compel
      Flight a'your own.
Or obscuring the light from indifferent stars
    As exemplars of base celebrity, conflicts
      And carnal wars through egoist tropes
        And shamming metaphors.
What even though, and this me Master doth deny,
    These very stars be our source,
Does not absolve that we evolved ta something worse,
   Than even these scorching hells
     What heedless abide their celestial course.
    What register this hell on earf.
The plague bring buboes what swell wif pus
      But beware, as these streets still teem,
   Our planet be such clot what swell wif us
And all earfly progress be toward a barren end.
    And now in me master's employ
Into these miasmas I oft descend,
   What I sees bestial visions John, hisself, not append.
What horror this Dutchman Bosch mere touch upon
   And as quick as I be seized, the evil vex be gone.
And as they fade away and
   But for the chill a'death be lost ta me
If these horrors in images could be told
    As upon me mind's eye
Into the light, day or night, they unfold
   What industry it be a the devil's mark.
A depravity a the sort so hot
    It makes one's blood run cold.
   And for me ta confess might bring back the stake
If not such vile reports get me tested in the lake.
   And Mr. Pepys confirm that such as he and I
What fancy a bit a'skirt do make
    Despite our different stations a congenial pair
   What seek ta snarl up in some missies underwear,
Though he be not loath ta beat
    And berate his own indentured lot.
But not me and not such that I be Sir Isaac's drudge

But I be a goodly nature ta share
His desire be it drink, song and ta pack his pipe.
    So Mr. Pepys be ta me a fellow in all things
From how a dandy rides or his flageolet
        Makes a cunny sing.
    Or witness London's conflagration
Or runs the Royal Fleet on the public weal
    What the Dutch defeat,
            Yet be spared by King's Appeal.
    And all on his visits he confide in me
A the court and parliamentary treachery.
And growing weary a'me secrecy,
    I divulge me visions of a doomsday.
  What Sir Isaac's labors be the source
What Mr. Pepys make light ta relate
        I be in good company
  For some Odysseus and Aeneas
      Make such a rash foray,
          And there be the well-imagined course
A heaven, hell and purgation
        A this Italian Alighieri.
    What is ta say wif all do respect
        What he commends
These gents write what doth na more
        Than make light
    A me troubles for a lap frough Hell
        Not give me fright
But a far more ghastly harrow be me plight.
    Certain, books be replete what ape me visions.
What be real and not some fantastical conceit.
    But likened ta a wormhole what traverse
A hundred pages of a scribens ledger,
    Wif passages obscured by the breach,
The very numbers eclipsed wif a burrow,
    What suspend the wage a'me immortal soul,
        Brought to me fevered brains,
    Be as I inspire me master's acrid banes.
        For it be not for my soul I grieve
But for all souls what in comin' times

Breave far worse, I beg your leave.
What me Master and Pepys argue frough the night
    Whevver a bloke is to roll one six in six
        Or two sixes in twelve
Where each toss be of a different bone.
        Rich men's games,
What for me a seven be my delight.
        And postin' it again and again ta set me right,
Ta buy the misses a bit a'cake or custard pie.
        What me gamblin', the ol' hen and me
    Don't see eye ta eye.
        More if there be a bit a'laced mutton
            Follow a good hand.
What wif craven fumes and Christian folly ta vex us
    Whilst me master excise much of existence
Ta seize upon some congenial bits
        What be not the sum a'anything
    And contrive a'moorings what won't hold
Such that a discord a'material bliss and
        Spiritual angst be bold upon us,
    Rubbin' up ta bespeak a'the apocalypse.
What the earf not be the center a'the universe
    That very conceit doth replace
The center wif it's foster race.
        Ta forge a great chain
For in the order placed upon all creatures,
    Upon the angels and upon man himself,
        And the manacles remain.
Me master say me best fortune
        Be a bein' born so low
    And so odd a mien and speech,
And alien ta the academies' warrants a debate
    Nor possess a reckoning by which ta calculate.
What intuition prove but numbers' surrogate.
    Take care there be no notice a'me heterodox in
Any quarter what concern witches and warlocks
        And the burning stake
Or ta be drawn and quartered by a team of oxen.
        Yet me master holds not Jesus

In as high regard as the father,
    And the Paraclete even less.
What wif me master's reknown
    Most readily comes ill-fortune
What the prelates seize his property,
    Stay his experiments,
Even rouse us common folk
    Wif our pitchforks and torches.
Fancy me haulin' Sir Isaac before some capon
    Like Bishop Gibson.
Would that not be a supernal joke.
Ah, the lovely, un-Christian invectives
    Sir Isaac would invoke,
Upon us what wear his imperious yolk,
What now enjoin, me mind in spiraling flight, -
    Enjoin him what curse and jape,
That he not choke on his hitch a'rope,
    So precise parceled it perfect suit his neck,
Would that the universe be so circumspect.
Ah, Sir Isaac, I will not piss and moan.
    Indeed, you saw other world's,
    And beggared them through this one,
    But never saw your own.
For what be worvy in us, you agitate
    Ta hear What be it earth's fate
    Be bandied by a bit a'numbers.
What for us folk it be but a few lifetimes
    What by god's word and Newton's,
    It be cast very late.
You do indeed do god's work
    And thus inspire an apocalypse,
The selfsame, no doubt, what John
    And Daniel doth predict.
And such be so that you bandy about
    By your own account
    Our denouement's true date.
By god's words and their sums
    You abet our earthly fate.
Prophecy resolves through invention.

Yet ya see no folly in such recourse,
    As reverse engineering the universe,
Maggots what gnaw the bolt a'heaven,
    Such what appear be the pinprick a'stars.
What wif the end matched by the deed,
    There be no need a'epics and poets,
For once taken apart and denoued
    Immortality despairs a'the heart.
There be no need a'beauty but what
    Reflect the mathematical arts.
Time like an arrow and the arrow, a needle
    O some fine but fleeting tapestry.
    A patchy age what can't abide its rage.
In a fevered dream enormous grey kettles
    What belch forf steam,
And contain enough stewed eel
    To feed ten regiments a'the queen.
But be not the offal in the pot, Sir Isaac, me and you
    And all the lads and ladies a'Woolsthorpe,
    And the fair folk a'Grantham and the hills beyond.
These night terrors I endure
    Noddin' off, as I do, just outside your door.
Time has come when one may
    Fashion fevers into prophecy,
    And prophecy into fateful circumstance.
    What these omens I see,
Be no pikey's divination,
    Be not a premonition,
A sign impending just for me,
    But for all what mortal be.
What triflin' ta leave your mark,
    It upon the face a the earth be struck,
    And left ta its appending dark.
And as soon as I be a scalder, I be a prophet too
    What not be born ta shape any man's destiny
But see it clear, as by caste, I be lashed ta you.
    Butt a'your jokes.
    Mutt a'your foul temper.
Grousin' in me mongrelese

Wif me kith under the ruddy apple trees,
   Didn' I spit out many a cure for you.
What do your diabolicals grace for god's sake?
 I'd sooner be buggered by that rake,
John Wilmot, than take another a'your sermons
     About god and his harmonious creation
   From one who accords nature but the
The wisdom of a puffed up, virgin potentate,
What such a marriage be a quarrel
Wif Gaia and end in bitter divorce,
For it seems, you despise our shared nature,
   No less than I or Hooke
       Or the Earl be of our nature born.
     And by artful cunnin' plot a course for murder,
As sure you plot the earth's orbit about the sun.
   And if, Sir Isaac, ya can't divine it, more's the pity,
For your kind be bound by invention,
   Ta counsel royal butchers
What wif evil intentions beyond fire and plague,
     Raze and desolate many a city.
You sir, in the service of a mere mortal crown
   Fancy Nature dead, dissect, all stripped down.
Indiscrete discretions, a stealthy shadow
     Of a Promefeus unbound,
   What demand fealty but deflect thy own
For only the Father merits your throne.
  As we be bonded, penned and cooped,
And naught but our wretchedness we own.
    You brand our lives this or that,
  So when we hear Wilmot speak a 'nuffin',
   Out of loathing we hear him speak a'you.
"Nuffin'! Nuffin'!!
    What dwell'st with fools in grave disguise"
What wif light throw dirt upon our eyes.

: Isaac Newton's Scalder, Abraham, Prophesies the End of the World

PART II: Elegies to Lost Ancients
What's Written to Endure enriches its value in the now.

Destiny Deals from the Bottom of the Deck
(for Albinovanus Gaius Pedo: In Memoriam)

Though of primordial Roman stock
I have no recollection of you Pedo.
Nor can I draw from history
        Tales of mates lost at sea,
    All salt scourge and chum for memory.
So in your lost epic when a gob laments,
        "The gods call us back.
Forbid us to know the end of creation with mortal eyes."
        Still lodged in my schoolboy's sanctum
Of what seemed an eternity of Plautus and Terence,
    Within whom the vulgar endures
            Ageless as a mortal constant,
I realize in Latin your surname means
            'I fart' in the second declension.
Pedo, pedere, pepedi, peditum;
While roughly suggestive of the erastic arts
            Of my Jesuit pedagogues.
    That through this most common portal
There might linger about poetry,
        Including the vulgar and the pederast,
 Something immortal
        Within our tempered solar annuity.

As my aged hull takes on water
    What do the alarums of ancient deities auger,
Where as in the Ancient Mariner "no wind blows"?
The gods "forbid us with mortal eyes the boundary of nature,"
        The world's verge.
Blessed Hoelderlin sussed but through the Word
        As a beast in its perpetual bearing.
            Socrates' oracle, both celestial and insane,
        Where in madness dwells the patient divine.

Tiphys of the Argo for whom a myth abides
   That the "symbolic subjugation of the sea,"
      Is prelude to what forecast declares such to be.
The first helmsman and the first boding of chaos
     As the prow of the Argo torn from the land,
   Moans low at its moorings;
  Then the death rattle of paradise,
    That grasping men call ignorance.
A hard, irrevocable reckoning embarks
    When bow slips from berth
And ventures upon the cunning waters
    Encircling the earth,
   And unencumbered of custom,
And so warrant to calculation,
    The mortal days of mankind are,
Aped by greater and greater acuity, numbered.

    But what scrap of antique pedagogy?
   What immortal quest? A mere sailor's anguished manifest,
Weighs in but 23 lines so marooned by time and fashion
    That a dozen translations vie for favor
  Yet choose their own obdurate rocks to crash upon,
What when cast and bled out upon the sea
   Brought total loss but for thee,
  And thy epic's intimation of immortality.
As a child might pluck a drowning cat
   From the salt-foul tempest of a fuller's vat,
In his Suasoria, old man Seneca saved
 Lines which have survived to this utterly alien time.
Take for example, this schoolboy,
   Who fancied he would be immortal,
Yet unlike you, a brave Roman decurion,
  Toiled no sea, fought no battles, won no crowns,
   All reserved for earthly kingdoms
    And kingdoms to come.
Fearing he too would only serve to genuflect
   And become but a nameless back trod upon,
Bound by the most cruel and cunning among us
   By whom such crowns are won,

Each to all revealed as imperfect man or woman;
Earthly immortals that prove out all too human.

After all, Martial, Ovid, all agree,
  That the shard of your epic that remains
  Points to a poem that would bring you great fame,
Still you wisely waited to chide foolhardy Germanicus
  Until after the imperial bugger died.
  In night fits I see
Roman oars strain against the swarming crenels of a god.
  A world "Where day itself fled".
Neptune crushed the fleet at the mouth of the Ems
  And cast like kindling with
  Many dead upon barbarian shores.
That plot, "the symbolic subjugation of the sea,"
  Calculations and computations
  In exordium to take up oars.
For like two devil's horns, the Pillars of Herakles
  Are borne upon the Iberian light,
And far trespassed had the Roman fleet
  Desirous to meet up with the eight legions
  And recover the eagles of Teutoburg
  Lost when Varus was brought to his knees.
The Pillars that in Dante's Odysseus and
  Tasso's Carlo and Rinaldo would repeat
  "the great ambiguous symbol"
The ethos of voyaging, of launching a fleet.
Both birth and death. The beginning of the end.
And as Bruno himself in Ash-Wednesday Supper,
And our High-Anglican, St. Louis cum Faber poet doyen,
  Embarkation is damned as the exponent of sin.
But immortality did not dally in caution
  So with Tiphys's apocalyptic timer once set
  Only an immortal poetic voice might rally within it.
And Seneca doubts, "Of the voyage what was the prize?
The golden fleece – and Medea,
  Worse evil than the sea,
  Fit to be the first ship's merchandise."

Praised by Martial who below your studio
    Lurked nocturnal in his lavish flat.
Drunk, screwing, playing his music too loud.
And Ovid from his hill top villa,
        Both whose work survived the wrack of time.
A void cannot be read
  Nor from a mere 23 lines can immortality be surmised?
But thy fellows by their praise preserve thee,
        As this be praise we not easily circumvent,
And greatness at least is arbitrary to what is extant.
            And now, without the imperfections of the god's,
 Lesser works abide ad nauseam
And earth now teems with humming sepulchers
            Of pedestrian thought.
Schoolboys can hack an electric grid
And straightway immolate a species' collective id.
        But exploration as the Fall of Man,
Perish the thought.
            The prow like a dog's muzzle rummaging the seas
The utile part of man's nature accelerated,
        Honing its entropic proclivities.
And quite literally take flight
        With much ado from all quarters
            About the conquest of Mars,
Draping Gaia upon the God of War.

        The fugitives flee, Pedo,
    From your sole surviving insight.
    23 lines but a ravishing keepsake
        Found upon Seneca's portico,
Hardly divine, though tried not fledged
        With immortality and
            Ignored, and vile when not.
By observation of Roman legions already wary of viral man
        "as we violate with our oars the seas."
No postscripts of enlightened beneficence, we at ease,
    Our oars, styluses, brushes and keyboards,
            As Macbeth said of this new man:
                "Making the Greene one Red."

No current venture capital Cassandra abides his inner frog.
    The lesson the Enlightenment fails to account is
        Destiny deals from the bottom of the deck!
10,000 lines which in beauty rivaled Virgil,
      And an apocalyptic prophecy rages in the surviving 23.
    A sign? The core, the 'dark matter'
        Of mankind's tragic Newtonian flaw,
  "Dancing in the ruins of our own free will,"
      As the prep-school cowpoke snarls.
And certain not to disappoint, given such freedom to fail.
The rest, man, poet, epic and war, drawn down,
When shipwreck was not some
      Cinematic suburban metaphor.
Where so small, granular, I scattered spectra of an end,
      Far greater than my own.
And that wisdom unwise can warrant exile
      As certain as Galileo's cities on the moon.
So Pedo, where does that leave the Parcae and I?
I own no storied bridle and lance,
    Nor sea and shipwreck to lean upon.
What leverage are my words against Morta's snip.
    Shall I fall upon what sword?
      And hope under some blade to not rise again?
To go shrouded like a scorned Lazarus meekly to my end;
    My words refrigerated like a severed head.
      Intact, mortal, and unread.

Hermippus

Is there enough forensics to know thee, Hermippus,
    With your two-bit haircut whetting your dirk,
Coaxing a salute to some unattainable beauty?
Or your cottabus-staff
Discarded among the household chaff.
Your every image speaks of the old man I am now.
To a character in a lost play,
Dead centuries gone, yet not lost to the everyday.
What aliases have time and the dons given you
As your bones lie picked in some boyhood lyceum,
Left a wind-hollowed pan flute?
As from your lost play, 'The Gods' croon,
    While the Furies cup limpet shells for castanets;
Rattles that dance
            In the tattered remnants of happenstance,
                Out of place
In this tomb insulated with commodious tomes,
And read with the certainty the stars once knew,
        I call out to death and
He sparks me in you.

Oblivion is the whip and the spur.
Not to go down the dark entire.
But for a while, a humble bit,
    To transpire through some act or words,
A more ineluctable accord
Struck with impossible permanence.
    Where scribbles lost to their mortal stewards
        Burn for a time in this carbon sway.

Creophylus

That fumbler, Chronos, misplaced your epic,
   A gift from Homer himself
        For lodging the blind peripatetic
     That some claim was your son-in-law;
       A work to claim as your own
     Purchased by your discerning patronage.
So Homer to match your daughter's dowry
Recounts in his Sack of Oechalia, Herakles' siege
     Also to claim the daughter of a king in marriage.
Poets have for eons been the pitchmen
     For that mad son of Zeus whose
        Rumor shines through the parting clouds
    From a common theft or murder in the street,
 Or a chronicler of heroes, or demagogues fiery speech;
      With pilfered apples and rustled cattle,
And the brutish domestication ex anime of beasts.
Or slaying Hyppolita and knicking her corset,
Or recounting a half-divine stable boy's janitorial feats,
With the mob scattering to seed legends in the pubs.
And what of Oechalia we can but surmise,
And so we concoct
Through our cataracts of Callimachus
And Strabo, Plato and Sophocles.
Or Plutarch's Lives where Lycurgus in his travels
    "Had the first sight of Homer's works, in the hands,
We may suppose, of the posterity of Creophylus…
Scattered proportions, as chance conveyed them,"
As objects of worship, entertainments, payment for debt;
    Time rendered fungible as their fate.
And all of your other works gone too
Including the Oechalia,
This grant of Homeric immortality,
That neither earthly kindness
   Nor cosmic curiosity
     Could secure for you.

Theognis of Megara

Nietzsche rates you
  "A finely formed nobleman fallen on bad times."
 Yet, more than half, 1400 lines,
  Of your gnomic quatrains survive,
Cast upon my shore this very day.
All the carping about lost possessions and the changing order,
    Plutarch's comparison to Solon and Lycurgus,
       Of laws that can be overturned only
By the creator's death or exile.
No. Not by simply expanding the franchise, the mercantile.
Nor falling back on civility your fellows don't possess,
     Nor the prerogative that money privileges text
Such that a thousand poets of genuine merit
But with no purse are vexed.
For your palette and divan may have been lost at sea.
Yet like an infant messiah, over the ages
    Scribes have wet nursed your shard of poetry.
Even though your gods toss the wealth of the earth
Like a quixotic rocker ravages a hotel suite,
You equate goods with gods.
And such that, this 'good', your favorite word, remains
    By sheer faith in you and you alone maintained.
 And no largesse stains your station.
And though you endlessly invoke your sense of virtue,
And though acknowledging your wealth affords divine caprice,
You fear Chronos will cart your words away
And hurl them into the bonfire of your own sanity.
That more than fire or flood or any prank of the gods,
So appalled you are by the future complexion
Of Apollo's erratic acolytes
That your verse and days are spent scolding Kyrnus
    For the abject passion he gave your nights.

Tyrtaeus

For whom art and immortality meant nothing
But to rouse Sparta against the Messenians,
And for me to tinder your surviving fragments
Against the existing imperial order.
For Aristotle bodes, "Crushed by the burden of the war,
    certain citizens demand
A re-distribution of land."
And as the scuttled ship's values recalibrate,
No amount of gold without ballast obviates insurrection,
For hegemony is so bonded with bad faith, murder and theft,
That revolt is ineluctable.
But you, Tyrtaeus, privilege Sparta's common 'good'
And martial but an insect's aptitude.
So sans the tease of immortality. What be that to me,
  Thrown overboard into this post-Odyssean flood?
This open sewer of fetid, irradiated humanity, bone and blood.
Riddled with its fabled ordnance,
Value assessed to its claims for the temporary.
The craven arts cozened by their fiduciaries.
The Sphinx concludes mortal Oedipus's three-legged span
Where words play on, but not the man.
But when The End is buzzing in your ear, what immortality?
A thorough excise reveals no riddle,
Denying the portent of the Argo's slow apocalyptic fuse
       That temporarily cajoled the cocky Muse.
So rouse dead Sparta, Tyrtaeus,
    What yips and grunts are left to you
And your bloody nation.
In the face of extinction, how could your boy scout city-states
      And your petty land-grabs,
Murders and enslavements mean anything to me.
With mere chains and knives, gats and nines,
  Rumbling with the brood the next block over;
The Messanians, Argives, Arcadians, and Pisatans.
    And the odds? Oh, the odds on immortality are slim.
It took thousands of gangland murders in Chicago alone

To pen one immortal, Al Capone,
    And his fatal flaw, not murder, nor racketeering,
        Nor bootlegging, but the leg iron of tax law.

Bloodletting is as common as god's indifference,
So, Tyrtaeus, you're of no use to me.
And as folks from Leucippus to Einstein have noted,
Armageddons are built on the atomic scale
        Where I see, you're but an anchovy
        In the maw of a whale.

Ennius

Father of Rome. Who could see it coming?
     Even Greek hexameter could not preserve
Its Latin champion.
As Propertius "put his puny lips to mighty fountains
     He slaked his juvenile recitations on thee."
Your hirsute telling, the Annales, to rival Homer's,
But still shaggy with the Saturnian,
As remained the heritage, so much mocking livery
          Of your tutors and slaves.
Both the meter that Horace dubbed horridus
And your work abandoned;
Outpaced by Virgil's Aenead,
Poetry as polished as his marble herm.
   Then as Caesar set fire to his own ships,
And so, by the way, your epic burned.
And not at the hands of some illiterate Parabalani cracker
     Who after dismembering Hypatia
Tossed your scrolls upon her pyre.
And some lout knocked your block off
The only bust inscribed Q. Ennius
And to pour salt in the wound,
          Public school pricks everywhere
               Stammer gibberish translations
   Of what out of this bitter turn,
          These puny pedagogues learned,
To mock your epic 'The Anals';
          And only to confirm their shortcomings,
     Their lob for immortality
In sixth form anthologies of puerile, assonantal verse.
          Time has a taste for blood.
Twin tongues of zest and fire, they are.
Though hard to credit your fragments the equal of Maro's
          Or your gods that of the hick vandal
Amidst two such colossal defeats.
Or your chinless jaw which is given a facile trounce
By the Augustan's pretty face

Beauty exalted throughout the ages,
    Inviolable, the bane of logicians and sages.
A visceral assay still with us now for all to gauge.
But precedent of your epic time will attest;
For Pyrrhic is the war waged with mere forensics.
Your cast of words like stone bound fossils mired.
        Lovingly preserved but stripped of narrative and desire"
And what man hopes that he will be king of Square Rome?"
        The lamp of the Eternal City.
For the best dig deep and unearth the dead
While the worst dig and unearth a tomb.
Even your Thyestes is lost,
 While Seneca Jr.'s is storm tossed to Britain
Where Jaspar Heywood made a translation in verse
And Shakespeare drew on it for his Andronicus.
Satires, dramas, the epic of Rome, brilliant shards survive.
        But time has tied our hands.
            Who can make a case for you?
So what of our judgment for one once, as Cicero says,
        "the most quoted, admired, criticized, and revived."
 Time has a taste for blood.
            The laurel falls to the one who survives.

Praxilla
(for Chris Vannoy)

Give us a song, Praxy. A slobbering, Dionysian swill.
   A wine-soaked tune of fate and folly.
I care not if I be amiss and
Lay me sweat soaked head in your lap
And look up wif me gap-toothed smile
      Hungry to sop a deep wet kiss.
    Blessed bawd panned by Aristophanes.
What us riff-raff applaud your bardic acuity.
And a bronze by Lysippus, no less,
Your anthems to wine and Bacchus much esteemed
What lasted? Only the first 4 lines of your hymn to Adonis
  Etched on a shard of pottery
Of the mid-fifth century BC.
Your verse be lost but your Temple be the pub.
   Your altar where we're nourished at bar and rail.
And drink is dear and us sotted flourish.
So swing wif me Praxy about the floor.
     What be shanty or a pratty sailor's ballad,
A song oblige a rig or a cup.
    So let's roar from the rail, a hail and fair weather,
And drown our wine dark sorrows, puttin'
Our backs into a Chrestien blokes Odyssean oar
Or echo Homer and Ares and the gods a'war,
Raise a cup and ape the ocean's roar
Forsakin' home for some foreign ness
What didn't cotton ta us then and don' namore.
And barroom laments sans Zeus's thunderous baritone
And the myth a'Tiphys,
What crack the alarum a'leavin' sake and shore.

But for Immanuel's morbid drippings
And ta the altar borne,
Wine now be riven from the god's.
And Chaucer's Pardoner begs your indulgence
A lecherous thyng be wyn, and dronkenesse

Ful of stryvyng and of wrecchednesse.
O dronke man, disfigured be thy face!'
What be the ruddy flush a'the Gaelic race
What voyage but a bit a'Dublin
Yet journey's song be shipwrecked upon such a place.
A return, a drunken homage to the gods
And to the devil just in case.
What it be Jimmy the tenor on the rail
Or the Caruso of Rock on the juke,
And na stone and clay
But wood and sawdust upon the floor.
Or 'Thar she blows' at a flourishin' fluke
Or poor Finnegan who
"Fell from the ladder and broke his skull
So they carried him home, his corpse to wake,"
There be you, Praxilla, make no mistake,
Even though we have beggared the gods.
Though lost we still educe your reverie,
Ta spirits affirm and death rebuke.
The refrain a'the wine dark sea
Be but that salt watery pits of oblivion
When in our cups we brood a'pain and misery
And death's anchor drags us down
And we drain our pint before we drown.

Hipponax

Agon A/1:3A
All sinew, Hipponax has grown fat on his hatreds,
For his jabs and left hooks are equally fatal.

Fragment A/2:4 Bupalus and Athenis
Narcissus at the theater weeps wif laughter as
Hipponax's combinations crush Bupalus and Athenis,
Til so battered with words
        They twin the homunculus Castor and Pollux.
Worked over in his mother's womb,
Such his countenance be of melted wax
Wif but the rudiments of a face.
        Jagged teeth that let no song pass and
      Chin and cheek pierced with hog bristles
          That stir the heart to predispose malice.
        What the sons of Archermus render him true
A monster cloaking another within
Lethal as Archilochus.

Fragment A/3,B Pharmakos
Hipponax, a pox of body and mind
      A pestilence that breached light,
Destined for the Pharmakos.
Gob ugly in both shape and speech,
Soggy contempt wif Aedes' sting.
All evil of men manifest in his words.
Did not his pallet of Stygerae
Offend the Keres such
That after passing him in the street
Some became palsied at the sight,
All the Ephesian toddlers caught the sniffles,
      Boners were suddenly hard to come by,
          And the turnip crop was wanting.
Proof enough, such omens,
So say Athenagoras and Comas,

Guardians of the lethal apocrypha of Archermus's sons?
  Even lancing this boil from Apollo's ass
    The gods may not be appeased for fortune,
      That our torment will become as butt ugly
As its source.
A more repulsive design mere Ephesians cannot fathom
    Explicit in the repulsion of his words
And acts as he and his mangy Aphrodite
Guzzle wine from a bucket.
So lead this Hipponax beyond the city's walls,
Place cheese, barley cake and dried figs in his hands
And beat his pocky cock with squills and thorny briars
    Until his cries appease the furies.
      Let the pipes snigger to the melody of the fig branches.
Then stone him, cut him into pieces and
Burn him on a pyre and scatter his ashes
      And crown his tomb with thorns and thistles.

Fragment A/1:3 Ephesus
What is the city of Ephesus to do
Now that Hipponax's play, the Crow's Await,
    Has flayed its soul?
Broadcast its depravities and vices to the world,
    Exposed the peoples' willful concealment.
  They have shaved their heads
And pierced their eyes with styluses
Handed out by the synegori
.   His haunches ripe below his blackened elbows,
 The magma of his words loosed
      Like a blast from Hephaistos' backend bellows.

B/1:C
Hipponax's doxie's got a nice ass
But for the boils
That surely arise
From the venomous kisses of her lover.

: Isaac Newton's Scalder, Abraham, Prophesies the End of the World

B/2:C
For all his love of rough trade,
Artemon's utensils remain undamaged.

Momus B/3:B
Touched by Momus, my ass.
Hipponax and his bitch roll down a hill
While fucking in a thatch privy.
Little wonder the Ephesians dispensed with his services.
Who's going to clean up this mess?
While, shitsmeared, he and his whore,
        Roll around in the market
                Coiled like two mangy vipers.

Peisander

Peisander of Camirus, who gave Herakles
That cave man look;
Lion skin about his loins and churlish club
Like a Louisville Slugger hewn of ragged wood.
That Alley Oop pose much in comic vogue today,
Internalized by a cartoon culture,
          That has spliced aping with vulture.
Enduring, though as Clement claims your tale,
        Albeit but that the Labors are 12,
From the Nemean Lion to the Augean Stables
     To the Capture of Cerberus.
            All else pirated from one
Pisinus of Lindus, more lost to time than even you.
Neither text survives. Pisinus not a word.
Peisander but 3 shards;
Two from the Scholiast in Aristophanes
And one from Stobaeus.
But when extant the Alexandrian Grammarians
     "thought so highly of the poem
That they received Peisander
Into the epic canon together with
Antimachus, Panyassis
Hesiod and Homer."

Is it enough to endlessly compete in Elysium
        So myriad be the affairs of the gods?
To route Eupolis and Pindar from Olympus
To take the laurel and dispose of Agathon and Sophocles.
Or witness after your burlesque of the mocking
Archilocus, his abashed ghost dangling from a tree.
Those contented with mortal judgement;
Jousting for time's sullied perpetuity.
As, in accord with Caecilius of Calacte,
Menander to Philemon
     "Are you not crimson with shame

Deemed victorious over me?"
As for those among the living
        Who fashion Fortune's indifferent victory,
Hold forth out of necessity but surely mistaken,
We salt with heaven's weeping
        What on earth is utterly forsaken.

An Open Letter to Anaximander and Eratosthenes:

The end is near
So let's suspend belief for a moment and suppose
That you may be relieved to hear
That in the not too distant future
There will be no one left to compose
A poem about the demise of your work,
For there will be no one left at all.
Extinction has been embraced
With willful ignorance as the accelerant.
A populist premium has been placed
On the very techne that is the apocalyptic operant.
Reason and sentience are the
Twin burdens of our overmatched race;
The euthanizers of the planet.
Or as Anaximander
"anything that disturbs the balance of nature
does not last long."
No surprise that a techne utterly subject to the binary
Has been backed like a lorry full of rotting offal
Into such a scholastic docking;
Either extirpation or algorithmic perfection.
A bloody cross or the head of a pin.
Soon that planet that you, Eratosthenes,
So lovingly measured in stadia
Will not have, as Nature abides,
An anime on it that gives a conscious good god damn.

The irony being that consciousness is
'What done-in the one what did'.
Dependent on the anonymity of numbers,
Awareness proved to be a mere poultice,
Even as our mathematicians decanted it
Pouring draught after draught of the sweet bane.
The planet itself being an insensate entity,
It was beyond meaning, so was not meant to be

A conscious thing merely implicit as a prevailing proxy.
      An indicator of a feckless strategy.
Tiphys might say, 'Too much rudder
not enough sail for perpetuity'.
As you Anaximander wrote:
    'Whence things have their origin,
Thence also their destruction,
According to necessity;
For they give to each other justice and recompense
For their injustice
In conformity with the Time's ordinance.'
The spade bites below the root.
And the species withers.
And more so with a Bamford back hoe.
As straightaway and irreversible as that.
God will be dead
Extinguished in the minds of his or her creators;
   So our Nietzsche will no longer
Be called upon to confirm or deny.
All dualities and taxonomies will be moot.
  Nature's mangle will no longer
Be mocked by Fibonacci.
And equilibrium will express its true self,
        Nothingness.
Bacteria will rummage through our bones
And, if they could, mistake it for hospitality,
Even as they didn't while our flesh loamed the planet.
    Eratosthenes, 2200 years ago, you 'measured'
Our planet's girth,
And the distance of the earth to the sun;
What our instrumented eyes see as near exact.
Now, our machines celebrate the Enlightenment
     Drift into the sterility of numbers.
And so, so must we.
Before the vamping strength of string or nano,
    Why act like the Luddites and not let go
Until flayed and hoisted upon the gallows
For crimes not of the imagination
But those which so indentured follow?

Columbus read of your calculations, Eratosthenes,
But chose Toscanelli's corseted route,
With its golden bosoms pushed out.
The more proximate the riches,
        The more likely an Imperial grant
    For gold is the measure of all things.
  And now when the Street bell rings
It's clear it's algorithms, quantities,
For what is scarcity but borne of numbers.
 The real root of all evil, what Nature does not abide.
It's right there in the Tiphys account, exchange.
Here tonight watching Cassini's cartoons of Saturn
Pixelated caricatures right out of the funny papers,
The narrative as puffed up
        As the black ulcers in a Lichtenstein,
Corseting my mind for treasure.
I scan my book strewn, filthy room to weigh true
      What remains of you, Anaximander and Eratosthenes,
Among this heady ruin, disordered,
      In the orbiting dust motes.
  The waters have taken up Noah Numbers.
    And there abides no landfall in the gloom.

PART III: Serial Killers
The Butcher's Apron

I shall not let the sins of others illuminate me own
As to contend with the glory a me own vices.
And if sheddin' innocent blood does not speak of honor,
You shall not speak a'me.
A'this I be certain as the Union Jack
      Reckons the Butcher's Apron.
For I be Amy Dyer and I stand accused,
And there be some right in it.

My Georgie, god rest his soul, was a bricky lot.
Accepted the Queen's shilling
And served the Empire during the First Ashanti.
What this very day The Guardian headline
After thirty years of accord what one Kwesi Gyana
Some darkie cut purse in Governor Greenhill's favor,
Flee Ashanti agents what cross the Pra
Where our own Colonel Wilstad
      Thrash them heathen wogs.
Baby Farmers they calls us widows.
But what these poor girls ta do,
Tossed out by their dads, most like,
And second kicked down a flight by the state patriarchy,
What we do be under the New Poor Laws a'1834.
      So who be the butchers?
I say look ta Malthus and Bentham and Ricardo and the likes
    What under whose cold abstracts we all be buried;
  As innocent of cause as the bloody dailies
    What now herald me name.
 What these learned wags be enlightened
What be nay more than Draco incarnate,
  Sly about numbers and quantities
    As alike they fear not posterity
For their accounts be in good order.
And who are we ta question where the noble gentlemen
Of the House of Lords take their pleasure

And what extremes of life and death they fancy.
Don' our Mr. Milton give voice ta Satan hisself?
Through Empire? Ta "wage by force or guile eternal warre."
So what it be these poor lasses
              Ta brood upon passion's wink,
  So's ta tithe me ta dispatch their own flesh and blood,
          What be but denyin' the Imperium short a sight,
                Its pound and pint?
And don' I for a true pound sterling give them hope.
And be it no more false than our dear Queen
What curse her own brood,
So's as what's ta be done a'the bastards
And simples a'the nation.
Most I tell be lies but lies what these girls be grateful;
Where none wif me be no worse
              Than starvin' on their own,
And at close quarters and slow and searin' torment
Where none ground be found
But in drawn out horror and grief.
Mine be but given a dose a'Godfrey's Cordial and
   'Laid in a papyrus basket among the bull rushes',
What infant corpses bubble to the surface
      Among the bur-reeds
 That run the marshes a'the Thames.
Bagged and weighted though as they be,
I serve both mother and child.
            Here as I be bundled away in this dungeon,
Below decks guest a the Lemon Street constab'lary
What an order be met of a deeper compulsion,
What a rendezvous a'the state of things
And its glorious implements.
Don' think. Feel. What does it feel like?
        Ta strangle a wee one. Ta strangle 300.
   Not what words belie but
To us whose touch esteems the carnal.
I suppose I not be a'your common ken
   But as I reflect, in flashes and circumstance, then again.
What the deacon be affronted wif his grief and contrition,

And callin' me "child" what I jape,
    "I have a cure for that, reverend,"
And run me niggler cross me neck.
Nay. I not call it compassion any more than Mr. Peel.
    But I not slam the door on a girl's backside
But return her to her customary servitude,
Neither a'what made any promises
And none which promises much or ever met.
Behind the hangin' shed at Newgate Gaol
The wind whips the Butcher's Apron above the yard.
        For these crimes
    You just as well hang me from the flagpole
        As the gallows.

1: The Butcher's Apron is a pejorative term for the British Union
Jack flag, common among Irish republicans, citing the blood-
streaked appearance of the flag and referring to atrocities
committed in Ireland and other countries under British colonial
rule.
2: Amelia Elizabeth Dyer (1837 – 10 June 1896) was one of the
most prolific serial-killers in history, murdering infants in her care
over a 20-year period in Victorian Britain.

Ma Gein's Lullaby

Bleed like our savior, you appalling whelp.
Bleed when you do that filthy thing to yourself.
You're no better than the swine you loath to tend
With lust's house pitched in the sty of excrement.

These beads of blood and sweat be your rosary,
Harrowed as you are, wee Ed, upon this rack.
Such rank license signals your destiny,
With the stench a'brimstone splashed off your back.

To Hell you were born and in Hell you will stay
Til Satan comes to cart your carcass away.
For the demon will be all the salvation you'll know
Having had me tend the better part of your soul.

PART IV: The Gospel According to Simon Kananaios- Additional Monologues

Pazzus Ubatzi bemoans the chaos and death Mary Magdala's Jesus Hoax has caused

A royal cock up from the jump, ain't it.
What not betoke any thieves bones as this Jesu
And be done a'it?
    Clearly, wisdom be not imposed upon a procurator
As freely as folly upon the people.
        Who knows a bone
    What there not be its own rut a'teef marks on it.
Or ta scratch out the feast days a the Julian
    Where meat once meet the famish rake a the poor,
What their tongues go silent at the portal
        Whilst their rage be clotted wif fat.
Bit ghoulish start ta finish, a'that,
        What wif dem wee ones murdered ta spite this Jesu.
And blood in the goblet even if he be just havin' it on.
And doubt a bit a'good bread ta name it flesh.
And plunder a corpse a'its spoils for rumor.
            This give a bit a offense ta most folks
What trust the doubt in the dispatch a'dice.
What odds be a'such,
    And what account be this but anuvver Mifra,
Or Horus or Attis or Dionigi.
        And don't the dagos crucify us like we's rags.
    What by chance or solstice be born a'the same day
That life here and now be eternal sought by all us wankers.
        Here I be but a knob what waits the Roman guard
But I know the twin and Abbanes from out the Kush
    And he, Thoma, be that what prowl past Fish Gate
            Ta ramp hysteria in the gillies,
Wif Yeshua hard dead and bore off some wadi ta rot,
        Reasonable men suppose.
But people be amok
        A these hairy tussocks fetid wif guinea seed

That their sisters breed masihs a'dago archers
          What leave lions dyin' in the sand,
As well as another man's cod in his bed
          Ta spurt sons wif two tongues
And no patrimony but earned rebellion.
And that be Barabbas what sing"
I come not ta peace, but wif me sword"
          And be not pretty by it
Like this pansy Yeshua
          What be in league a'the Gamalas.
 Jude ta be offed and keep the brethren cranky,
     What epiphany Magdala thumbs down her Jesu,
It bein' time for a bold move ta top the till
          Til it be too cumby for a pikey haul about
And a lady need furnishin's and a roof,
          Don't she now.

But it be a cock up
          What abate many a pensioner from the rolls
                    At the nice end of a pugio
Or cinched face down upon the gibbet.
This bloody business a masihs,
What stand not an army but the people's will
          And wonder favor a'that.
What make allies a'them what would see them subject.
And knowin' as whole generations be a engine a'rebellion.
And pay themselves out as such
          That this dago curse be removed.

John Zebedee 2
(Hooked on the drugs concocted by Joseph Barsabbas, explains to
Simon Kananaios why Simon is the one that should memorialize
the crazy shit that's happened to the followers of Jesus. He's
oblivious to the fact that Kananaios will attempt to destroy Jesus
through his Gospel.)

For wifout curious curs, or sorcerers, and whoremongers,
        Murderers, and idolaters.
                Whosoever loveth the lie,
What sinner be ta slap and dowse me wake
        A'me sweats or chokin' a'me own bile,
As I be scourged wif pangs and bale a'the world's demise.

And Kananaios ask, "Who be this press a'foundlings?"
  And I, "They be what think the dagos come ta take him."
"And who ta be took? "
"What ask? Bloody Yeshi no doubt," says I.
"But the guineas be but Atilius and a coupla ruperts," says K.
        "By compare Yeshi's gillie's be many."
                So's I, "and many but shite a'the sword
        As mos' his fry be fey a'his will
What be a false coze."
"So John." K. summon "Be you baffle Pilato
                Be ripe ta off our genie?"
"Fuck no. But what it be a gent like you
                What be ta scribe our rebbi true
        And baffle his will what be a death beyond life?
He got somethin' in mind a'you.
But you be false
                What betray his franchise?
        Ain't you curious what be happenin' here.
        Somethin' you not know.
    Yeshi be clear a'his mind but his soul be mad.
                He's dyin' I think.
        He hates all a'this. He hates it…

The voices.
But he got plans for you.
          Na, na. I'm not gonna help ya.
You're gonna help him, man. Your gonna help him.
I mean what they gonna say, man,
          When he be gone, huh?
Because he dies. When it dies, man.
When it dies. He dies.
What they gonna say about him? What.
          They gonna say.
     He was a kind man?
He was a wise man?
He had plans? He had wisdom?
Bullshit, man.
Am I gonna be the one what 's gonna set'em straight?
Look at me.   Wrong!
You.
               You Kananaios.
For I be too battered and baked a'Barsabbas' elixirs
          What I be shadow boxin' wif angels.
And see rainbows 'bout an emerald frone
          What confound the fishmongers at their nets.
And beasts wif eyes fore and bung
          What a man be covered in boils and barnacles
Such as mine be a fond practice a'rue and stinkweed.
     I bein' acquitted higher than most what mop about
A golden bowl full a'god's wrath.
Torrents a'blood and bleedin' rivers and springs.
Darkness, fires, sores, vermin and drought.
What our masih claim ta be Sardis 'thief in the night'
What shake down said burg, Sodom,
               What under Tibi be rebuilt.
     Our rebbi wif his idle threats and select alarums
What get the people so cheesed off,
          Sore they not repent.
          As such be me incline.
          And they gather ta face the Thief at Megiddo
And not falter a'his barmy caprice.

And I stagger as me head be a crazin' glass,
A ashen world it doth impart
    Such that monsters puff and wretch upon our rebbi,
        What lady Magdala shew off,
A giantess a'horrific grimace.
    And there be a woman upon a crimson beast
        Havin' seven heads and ten horns.
    And be these upon beast or beauty I cannot say
Such be Barsabbas' brew and a fortune's tellin'.
        But that I prefer it be beast be so deformed
            As ta make me not go limp a'the tart.
I not claim I not be privy a'the true sayin's.
            I just not be a bloke ta sort such
From dragons and shanks bolt ta gullet, or
    Where the waters roar huzzahs as be a'Indi's shores.
Or be our Yeshi drippin' a'blood
    What be not what he impart mostly, nor be his gift,
But that others die in his sake
                    For want a'arms,
Callin' legions a'vultures what such numbers
            Shite a battlefield a'fine guano glaze
Wif so many dead ta stuff down their goozles.

But what import be it ta get our rebbi straight
            Where the broad bide us
And the bidin' be cardinal?
            What be this after-chance
What ta be as by Joe's rue,
            Heaven's Hell?
            I knock about the whole menagerie
And still be here ta slur me tale?
I mean I seen it what Yeshi babble on,
            Complete wif whore.
What me belfry do wonder as be fit
            A'what heady rue be in me blood.
For it be no bloody rood make me straight.

Stylos Kynikos rejects the idea that Jesuswas a cynic philosopher

What dog be this,
  But ta lend pretense ta be a dog?
It manifest a cur.
Be it this raven, Yeshua, what creep about Gadara
                For stock bits a Mennipos,
            As Diogenes and Crates be
  What his god kecks by spoliation and death.
            These that by their fetid acts
      Ministrate a notion what be not godly or dogly
As be this economy a letters in some parlances,
But namore but put the taint a'sin on our labors
            As we not so much labor
So as not ta be brush a'such evil.
Ravens and sparrows be a'this shite Yeshua.
            A fuckin' fief and fraud
What twist and pop upon the pyre
The very strokes a'the Antisthene a'stort.
For what a lily be ta a man?
                And if be so why the sparrows' cheep
What hail a pickpocket quick as a Mary.
            Yet who doth not spin go naked
And this we have seen as Diogenes piss and shite
      And go buff a'the thoroughfare
And gob the beards a'the rich.
And so the Dog bide Yeshua do the same
      And that he not render the poor a'their bequest.
  And what toss dice ta determine
      Not Barsabbas but Matthias
        And other tasks what be dealt by bones.
The rich be but sheep wif golden fleece
                And what they be fleeced by Yeshua
What be beggared by empire,
            Not beggared a'themselves
But a witless conceit what advance.
      And what the Sinope be ta chide a whore or fief
What be not keen ta seek him out who has naught

What they as he ta dine
Wif revenuers and Judies
      And other sordid publicans
As but accrue ta others what he has forsaken.
      The Dog waddle his tangy bung a'these
In the thoroughfare or at temple
      And all Athens amend its lust a fortnight.
And he beg a'Anaximenes but piss upon his boots
What Jesu's doxy see fit ta anoint wif oil
      For no bile a'the rebbi.
Aristotle enlight Alexi Magus
      What by turn mind the Sinope,
      As the Sinope boon the king but a smudge
What want ta stand clear a'his light.
And why chrism for none bear up this creed
      But tithe ta be borne up?
He too so borne a sop be a rag in the hot sun.
  The Sinope too be much reviled and much revered.
And I concede Athens had not Rome's foot up its ass
    But so better will ta lay low a'these guinea apes
Than ta get 'em pissed up about missin' a siesta
    What some wank cause a stir 'bout Herod's Gate.
That's just me thinkin' on the topic
      What have centuries wise.
And seen what blood rite and omens' tether.
And Cosmo the Sinope have it seem he but a bowl to dwell
  But it be the tortoise shell upon what this Yeshua strides
And a happy dog be its meat and claw.
      Not some simple wank
What got ta work through bile, blood and infinite sorrow
      Like a surgeon a'some decimate phalanx
To cupel a masih's ass in a golden chalice
      Or cauterize it wif Rome's light
As pity be a those what seek pity there
Enslaved ta an after life as they be.

Rockmiel
(Angered that the Romans won't
give him his reward for bringing them a prick
he claims belonged to Jesus of Nazareth.)

Bloody lot a'sheep fuckers
    Be Simon and his yardies and this Jesu ponce
What by his own hangin'
        Concoct ta topple Tiberius.
    Or what more ta props
What his ol' lady had a mind.
    And run the crow bait off
 Like it be resurrect or some such.
What I be called fraud by Pilato's own guard,
I what bring 'em this Jesu's dandy dooley
        What they might muzzle the gossip.
I 'spose the rebbi may got off ta resurrect
        Sans buzzuto, me bein'a reasonable man
            Wif me wif and where's a finance
    And what be the knotted purse string a this empire.
And that principalis, this Gatian,
  Say straight ta me mincers,
"How we tell this here pud be a fortnight hung
        What prick be aft the bung a'this Notzrim chap?"
I says, "Sergeant, what? The Christers
        Go dickless in Valhalla?
    Fuckin' bloody cut the crap.
        I been about the bloke.
What chippy take this girth but Magda,
    The miller's daughter, the one out Hebron?
What she be brought ta aver this be her boy's pecker?
And dun I be mongst these fiends at Gethsemane
        What bloody the bung a'that twink Amir."
    I knows this masih's bone first hand
What be free ta take me literal on said occasion
        When a copper take a turn ta wine.

I knows to you guinea wankers
        It be a bit Spartan for what we take a'masih's
 And a one what bespoke a'such love and affections.
    But what I be rightful ta five a'Tibi's mugshots
In silver stamp. So's I says, I did,
 "If you's be forfwith
Before me last bender done fog off,
     I be oblige nat ta report ya
                Ta one Atilius Publius Quintus
What keeps me in cups for the cloaks and daggers
     I done for him, if ya gets me drift.
A all these daft Jew masihs and they's crews.
I knows me market, meat and all,
    And true this be that bloody masih's kishka."

At what this Gatian shite frow me down a flight a stairs
        Likes I be a Roman proconsul
What take a lovely leap a'the Gemonian.
And the bloody kitts abscond me relic,
        What the sergeant call 'confiscate'.
    What a honest bloke call nick.
What they say be held in evidence
        What it in life be much hand ta mouf.
            Took for they's bloody Mifra, no doubt.
    What I catch that guinea crew drunk
A the Cardo I put a blade ta use and
        Finish me a bit a'empire
And the shites what square it off.
Be the labors a'Herakles ta secure that pecker,
What I dig faster than the jackals
    What me thirst be more dire.
And take a beaten from the badus
        For fuck up a'some bloody fealty
A them pikeys what thinks us lot got souls.
    Dun I know a bloke or two
  What would cut off their own for bit a'treasure?
But why this provenance,
        What this nancy principalis calls it?
What but he say they got a dung cart

Full a pizzle and parts,
What remain hid as mos' peckers be covered
    Ere the light a'day
       Lest they celebrate the night.
And what matters it a jizz blessin'
    If it forestall rebellion?
A brief shake a the dooley at the crowd
And declare it be the genuine.
    What thems gonna stand by their
       Buts, behooves, anyways and anywhere's
Considerin' the subject.
    What David raise up Golyat's nog and
Johanna and Serafina tell ya by John's,
What there be certain somethin' about a head
   No matter how stink ta rot.
      But a cob? That be for the missus
And a few twinks and twats ta warrant.
  What, this shite, Gatian got downright philosophical
What wif me head swimmin' wif his ordos and such.
   I got this bloody part at hand and no other play.
But I done beat off jackals and pikeys
   Ta arrogat it
So's the bloody kitts ain't heard the last a'me.
   What Magda vouch for me a'it
Bein' some relic a'her mister.
   Or his boys what be on the road a'him
    And be a bit frisky wif wine.
Or his ma, what doddle his dooley in the washpan,
Be eager ta atone a'his frauds and slanders
   What wif Roman lashes waitin'.
Some birfmark or scar what be uncanny
    Given me yankin' at the wank what I rap
     A jackal on its muzzle with me staff
    And make off under a badu thrashin'.
Bloody kitt marionette. "Take me ta Atilius
  So's we blanch this Jesu's false charter
And a Rome bofe Pilato and meself
   Pay our debts and fill our larder."

"One more word and I'll bury you in the Antonia,"
    Threat this Gatian prick.
"Aw fuck off," says I. "Pilato's game be rigged
    What nig over 5 silver drachmas
What he bleed out treasure a'all these hereabout."
And run off, I do,
    What them kitts make me own pecker
      Anon a'me
        In that dung cart.

Lenocinus Captio tells a rich pilgrim a tale

"Quiet down Mr. Barsabbas.
      Your puddin' cools at the sill
Whilst I be at the portico
    Chattin' up a gent what's got a purse
Ta challenge Goliat's scrote
      Hangin' thereby but a margin left.
Twin sacks
   As Cain's be Romulus and Abel's Remus
     Or as Didy be a'our Yeshi.
So hush while I chat up our pilgrim.

(Turning to rich pilgrim)
You want to know me, good sir,
     For I be very scribe to Kanon Simon,
Blind therein, groanin' ta gum his dinner.
     The same sicari what make dagger a'his pen
       Or pen a'his dagger,
   Whatever evil be ta sort,
      Be it aphairesis or ink well.
And depose them's what bear witness a'Yeshi ben Pantera
    By touch or smell or sight or word.
      What be his cozies and intimates,
    Cronies and coursers
   And other what upon he bore.
What come ta his flesh ta hang
     And what come by same flesh ta eat
An abomination like ta get one hanged
     If god or dago procurator's got a say in it.
Me blind master, Simon, be about all
     What desire ta ken that Yeshi bugger
What at full sight be at the side a'John the Baptizer
   And at the day a'the Nazarene's approach.
So these what follow witness
     What a true god and true church be witness
For fear a'false prophets a'rumor and discord

      Bond from their own dearth a'fables and lies
A'these transpirations we attest,
      As I mean Joe what make dilutes and potions
Through me and me through him,
      And deny we such portage a'god.
And as he be tempted by the devil
      Long before he made a parable a'it.
   A shaver what be the devil himself some say.
Late by gildin' outcomes as ta appear comely before his flock.
      And modest
    For a fable wif a bit a'indict a'the fancier be a parable
      What many fancy they see themselves.
For a good parable be kin a'Hypnos and ta strip a purse
    Wif a bit a'sparrow's chirpin'
Ta fortify the peckin'.
      And ain't we got meat and board thereby.
And be stout in our numbers
    And waves crash and the blood a'martyrs
     Is spilt in our name.
That this tale be a'two messiahs and a beard,
    One a denial
  What nevertheless be subject to bloody recompense.
And two, a pretty Magdala's contrive and tempo
    As she remain so Queen a'the cult
As she be gird ta mop and towel up the gore
      Lest glory seek ta buoy the bob and rise a'others
Or spark a schism what two pockets need fed.
    Like this Tarsus what be easy liberty wif the deeds a'others
And verbose as tales a'those
    What by his own sword cropped
     When he saw their gold then delivered.
A scoldy shite what those he make gaze up
   Find their cup empty a'the next swallow.

So make need a'me and me master,
    That thy pouch not purse thy back
Or bandits cut thy throat.
   Hear him and the true gospel.
The word a'me Master Simon.

Me daft rebbi claim he be the bell a'god
　　As your threadbare poet claim
Over cheese and maggots
　　　He be at the elbow a'Tiberius.

Joseph Barsabbas the so-called 14th apostle and the drug connect to Jesus and his disciples.

(What are scholars to make of the Joseph Barsabbas' monologue in the Canaanite Gospel? The monologue chronicles not only the life of Jesus, following quite closely the synoptic Gospel of Matthew but also that of John the Baptist but from the point of view of the disciples' main pharmacologist/drug connect, local narcotics being essential for the staging of the 'miracles'. Barsabbas's perspective describes a far more plausible and humane set of events than the Synoptic Gospels. The Gospel monologue of Joseph Barsabbas should serve as a balm and comfort to those 'believers' concerned with the absurdities and contradictions that make the original Synoptic Gospels seem so utterly implausible to potential adherents. If Jesus is the question, drugs are the answer.)

Our bloody procurator sort out our lit'le Jesus,
       Didn' he now?
    No mere stinkweed mirage
Booted at barb and quill
      Be that bit a guinea craft.
And here I hurl about me cell, a fly
    What don't know where ta die.
Be me wine but water
      And me water bereft a'dhattura
Such that visions not take me
   But ta set me down 'mongst me own stool,
     Me gut writhin' and twistin' ta wring a rag.
Prisoner a'love for what me gather ta hate.
     For I be a cooker a'Syriac rue what make miracles
   And what the eye see the mind negate.
And what wif rebbi among them some imbibe
   Yeshi as god what prospect frighted me.
     And he yet voice what habit the visions
   And me modus be not writ
Lest me hands and head be lent
    Ta the speculatore's knife.
Miracles be but theatre,

A bit a'rue, bunko, gossip and lies.
     A hydra when the people's put out
    Its they's bloody nogs what greet the sword .
So's I mix me stinkweed wif henbane quiet
     Ta limn the underworld and abide magic.
But too much heat applied leave a bloke
    Ta prattle what be aft his eyes
Or sojourn beyond what be before.
     Some wif dash a henbane and stink feign death
   As this be dhattura's sayin'
    I be what be 'sent ta die'.
Or heat and cool, a drizzle and dross by turns a brew,
    And plys a leaf and vines a hamal heated in a kettle
What savory brof send our masih ta Gehenna.
    Or soak a repast what the mob conceit they see
For lust a'what be known
    Beyond the eye be but gad a'Archimedes pi.
And doth proportion as a dream deceive but a longer pace.
    And apocalypse doth waft upon the breeze
Like a cipher what preclude the garble a man.
    So what be phantom fish and bread in heaps
     When the mind count the belly full
  Deceived as such as we served?
And healin' and sins abasement be
    On hillocks where but sheep gentle graze.

What cast bones for his cloak be me cast in lots.
    But shoot I craps and be out the franchise
     As I be cast out the twelve,
    Like I be but a bit a'dirty swag
Me what tend their visions in cups a'flowering venom
     And spin the mob as what be sooth.
    What merit be a pretty Matthias
     As I me potions work miracles
What waft manner a purse and purloin upon its vapors?
    Some be a'our imbibe.
What par boiled amanita and kannabos
    Be at table before his pinch in the garden.
     Some be our host. And some be bofe.

Young Johnny Zeb revels be a fly on shit,
          And what be a honey and locusts by dhattura
        What be at the body from above
Like a dove divin'. And by our drunken fraternity
          Jesus be baked and gad off
Into the Negev much arrant and returned
       Eased back a'me arts wif a purge a false hellebore
        What was fit ta end his triflin' anon.
Demons be a his own kindlin'
          As hunger stalk our slikey rebbi into the brush
Where he tramp luf and saina for milkweed and muscar,
      Not knowing badu ways. And jimson
Which flourish more the mind than belly
        And coax death closer
Havin' 'bout its own inspiration,
        The expiration a those what does it.

     Brew me a trim bit
A'henbane, datura and Syriacan rue.
     What nasty bit a'bizness we six imbibe
Be a Yeshi, Maffew, Stink, John and Judas,
     That any what toss be touts a true transpire
As oblique and clouded be the parable a'any messiah.
       He be not a divine
      And thus our blame be a'this knowledge
For'pon Herod's death revolt be at Sepphoris,
         Judah ben Hezekiah what be Judas Zealotis
A the House a David what
      Plundered palace and armory.
        What interject the archer Panteras Tenth Fretensis
Be one a Varus's dago thugs
      What run the righteous ta Nazaref
        Where he fancy Maryam, and she he.
And they coite amongst the staves a 2000 crucified.
        And thus a kit swine Juda and Jesus be sired
     A Joe's lusty second frau, Maryam,
         As Amina be dead a third harvest anon.
       Salome Zebedee be the mid-wife, kinswoman a Mary,
What twins kept close the twins a'her table and

Curse bofe dem mutts, I suspect kenin' a shine
    A their wreck and ruin.
For Jesus be twice the improper geezer
    What filf make a'Cain
        As Abel ta Juda.
           Or simple ta its guinea fate be a Romulus
    To a fuckin' Remus
For ta nature's buckle nations and their
        Fables be twined and twinned,
Nuffin' new under the sun,
        Even unto the seed a'this dago curse what be upon us.
        And what play went bad at bones, didn't
The rebbi cede his runt bro to the slaver Abbanes

And Jesus take up Pelasgi's stage,
        Prate a'Sepphoris's playhouse
      Lackin' the stones for cold mail
Yet desirin' his ass be seen in it
        Be the chain but be a stained and pitched burlap
What might be set ablaze in contest
        Amongst angels and footlights.

John be pinched and done in.
        So's we's up Capernaum way
     When we saw death though we
        Be high atop drunk
And any other state what not urge agile flight
     What with grousing we keep discomfit
And he fink water be beneaf his feet
        What be but drydock.
     So's the rebbi looked for shills
And thus come upon two rubes be fishers, Simon and Andrew,
      What saw us stagger toward the light.
    And the two the rebbi promised slaves
      Be they fisher a'men
What nets be less whips and shackles a'his word.
     And they drop their nets
What Matthew and me soaked at local for a few quid.
    And James Zebedee and wee John

What took right ta the toke
What revelation be a plenty function to afright the afflicted
          Be but garbled tale by ingest a'stinkweed.

          As grubs be the manna a'many a wanderer
As we sat 16 down and I stirred me potion killin' none
          Ere the devil not test me skill
And the rebbi promise heaven a'those what suffer demons
          And fits and pains such that much need a weed
Ta cloud eyes a sensible oratory a'creation. That dark be light,
          Or crawl ta walk,
          Or some wump wax a new tail
And crowds and coin be at our behest.
               And the procurator's man Atilius come by us
And offer 10 cisterces ta punk the crowds lay down their arms
          What be but hoes, sticks and axe
          And our rebbi ta the Mount forestall honor
What these defeated Essenes
          Rather swallow shite than gold.

And what source a bliss be a'these beatitudes,
          But bewitchment what any procurator hush the rabble
Special what already be a bit cowed by show a'arms
          And what jimson incense anoint.
          This be terror's reason, what
Blessed be them's what be like lambs,
          For that put in mind of a savory kabob
          And a few masihs been about
          What be finished on a spit
          Be Judas Sepphoraeus and Matthias Margalus.
Or be daft the righteous what think
          A just recourse wifout what first course be a'arms.
          Not wif these dago bastards.
And bounty be in heaven indeed
          As the kitts oblige many wif or wifout cause.
And wif our rebbi talk be sway a'the tongue, not the brain
          For salt wifout flavor do still revive
          And be key a'this revolt
          What glanced wif flint be a bolt a'flame or

What glossy art Didy recur a'his indenture.
        And this be that light what shine before man
And kitt fuckin' legions ta man and light abort
        What gone blind and stumpy from its glow.
      And more the mumbo jumbo a beyond Indi
        As beyond our gnosis,
What be the rebbi's purpose but be under Didy's tutelage?
      And our rebbi talk the Tanakh
Lest his vices attest his treachery.
     And don't this be a despicable bloke what I follow,
So pure a'evil it breed some love in likes a'me
      Born a'contemptuous guilt and flight ta jimson
       For he accuse and extort as
         Though the Antonia be at his behest,
As weak men fear what in the strong be but a jest,
       Prologue to a proper beatin'
As I once be ta dry slap the bloody heilige melt
      For same a'me what be about mine
What I fear for by the hand a'this madman,
      What all smiles wif fey stroke strike thee dead.
And he damn what insult his simple twin Didy
      What fetch a few bits from slaver Abbanes .
But it be Didy what not be curled wif heat
       And self-made and prosper a'his studies
        What be not chains but angels when iron's ta flesh,
Though these crafts be horrid daft but for a dose.
      And rebbi fuck his femmes as not have ta bear in his heart
       Tis sold other what be also a'his ma.
And boy's bung he bear upon his prick
      What be blind ta his word
Lest he stagger before the Philostene's
     In chains a'his own smithie and
      As manner a'salvation,
    What be be better than the if be
What needs test the rabbles limits
    Lest a wit among them
Wif his own filf upon his mudgy
      Comes forth ta crowd the donna.
And in this ain't I falsely sworn

      Him what swears but oaths what find comity wif me nature,
So's ta transit black ta white and know what I possess
      Lest such judgments what be weighed false
In truth be not so.

And not by eye or toof be easy a'his ta say,
      What be the dry slap doin' and the borrowin'
Lest Johanna crack him crossed the mug
    For his wanton choosin' and laborin'.
Recommend be what him what don't want, don't do.
      Ovverwise prepare ta witness Jesus Layabout turned out
By one or more what hammers and plasters wif him
      Or thereby comes ta rob and thieve
And our enemies what
      So loved would gladly send us to Hell,
Or whatever home reside beyond the point of their pilums.
      And whose father be this, but mine be Barsabbas
And scaffold be about peak ta sky as he get.
    Or Matthew what love the tithe before the man
Yet we a his ta love the man before the tithe
And listen'a our bellies growl praise Hosannahs a'such perfection.
And alms, what give?
      I be a'no franchise what alms be given ta pride.
So there me alms be in secret if ya's askin'
      And of a great many like demons out the eye
A'Johnny Zebedee bibin' the loco
    And room and door must precede furtive prayer
What anyway be outside this father's heaven
      Or creed a'any Stoic.
Not sure about Epicure
      What not bane lost a'me master's purse
But for the piety a'some close
      What our rebbi tendered as vig
Ta the piety a'acolytes wif property.

And what this life be more than food
      What make his whole body bread and bloody wine?
And if I be a bird a'the air are not me flights a'sewin'
      And me retreats a warm clime a'reapin'

As our lord be as dotty as a rock.
        And be I not a'more value but by me snares
And savors and aromas a'the kitchen.
        Or lilies? Fuckin' lilies! Be he preach ta lilies
Lest he want for disciples
        And be we not anxious starvin' amongst the posies?
And our families left famished in the fields
        That many a'time we broke to provide
Only to go back lest in these times
                Our rebbi's grift be not upon us ta provide,
And this perpetual going forth to starve for our own sake
                Or left behind to starve in place
Bond our spirits by that belly our rebbi so eschew.
        And why forego me judgment
When the ass a'it be so clear in me face,
        For it be not speck and it be not eye
And log a'not the flowery kind what disavow its cubby.
        Not the kind what dance upon our rebbi's tongue
But so to produce no less a stink.
        And I loves me dog, Apollo,
And what's got pearls to hurl upon anything
                After these kitt thieves
Lest there be alchemy in me diet
        And monkey in me manners.
"Ask, and it will be given you," and ain't I
        What be six months in arrears and whence me knock
Our rebbi be stabbin' his Magdala wif his celestial pilum,
        Wif his deep grunts what serve us all
And her cries what, no doubt, attest to our liberation.
        And what this bring about
                What suppose ta abandon us in heaven
And ain't hide nor hair for millennium
        Be likened ta me love for
        Me missus and me toddles.
Babes what speak more honest than our rebbi
        And more certain than his god that be mute
                As he only be a'signs and horror.
        There be but one god in times a'tyranny
And he be a wroth a'the condition a'his own

      And shows the wide gate that his beloved may rush in
And slaughter those oppressors.
        And times me and the rebbi comes to words
A'this illusion a'peace and love and its narrow ways
        What be more ta nibble at purses
          What be a sparrow's fare.
And he be the false prophet though keep his cohort fed
      Lest not his good tree regard the belly
        As the evil one do not.
Be I abide content a me figs.
        But I pick me teef wif a thistle
      And what be wedged thereof be meat.
      And what be cut down cook me meat.
So thistle be a utile sign a'feast too.
      And that be me preachin's
        Sound as any shite a'Yeshi's.

So's he threats me wif dis wifholdin' a'salvation
        Sayin' he bad mouth me ta his pa.
And I says, your father's Panteras, a dago cunt,
   So better fuddle your catamite hysterics
      Before I crack one crossed your gables.
And be it rock or sand, stink weed bind him to me
      As I be its master and thus his.
For such a house as on rock he never had
      But in loco fever,
What he ought not ta forget
      Lest I cut him off
      An' leave him live in his own head, foolish prick,
What nailed his house ta air
      And come ta dwell in it, didn' he.
   Like a pesky bat tacked
      What's sucked its last humor.
An end what them crowds be
      Better tutored by the scribes
What wifout his circus pick their pockets.

And what wif me potions
      Many deluded what see a healin'

Or what appear ta rise out the grave
What from me brew
                    Fall proper dead and ta their dreams
In a fortnight from potence a'what be fore said.
            Course rumor be our pranks be cream when
Guinea prick be in the butter
            And boils be fine as fleece
What shew themselves a'the priest
                    What be alarmed
        As charlatans the desperate abide
                    By adapt the temples stock and trade.
And fear ta answer ta them dagos
            What be about gold and blood
And commitin' that ordination ta the world's adamant.
                    And certain show no bit a'patience for our colly capers.
            Nor muse what Isaiah be fulfilled a bit as the stupor last
But death and disease will out and abashed
            All remittance be gone
Ta our shitheel, pikey bellies.

And where he lay his head be nowhere
                    But the between the crème thighs a'Magdala
That such reverie not be snapped
            For sake a'some bloke's dead padre,
                        But join and conjoin.
            What our kitt tossers call carpe diem
As be bosh a'one them dago poets
        But more probable a keen a'some odd Pelasgi.
And what this one want all else ta defer his pussy and beer
                    Such he be in his cups and worse dry.

            And in flight passed out, or rebbi, amidship,
Waking ta calm sea ta claim his dream settle the storm.
        'And what dream be that, master,' says I.
                    And he, 'Oh Barsabba. Ye a'little faith.
Be sure I not dream a'thee
            As be it dilly what conclude thee,
                    For me thoughts be not your thoughts
And your mind ta mine be as a monkeys

Or like unto some stolid ape."
This from he that had eyes for nothing and ears for less.
What see swineherds frantic wavin' and bloody callin',
But still drive their sole meat over a cliff.
The cat what swallow the canary,
He oblige all grins and like,
What takes a pig's nature
And mistake it a demon's possessed.
And honest men wronged pled the magistrate
And didn't that folk cast him out their precincts
As he did a'their bacon.
And fortune they not eat him
What bartered he be bread ta the menu,
Fuckin' daft sot.

And Matthew be a proper piece a'work, did'n he,
What sit down ta table wif the rebbi.
And the Perusim say ta Simon, 'Your master feast among dunners
And Seduqim agents what bruise and tithe our labor.'
And he in wont a'the master's jingo wager,
'Sure he be but ta know their ways
Ta be better about the business a cachin' they's souls.'
'And what be the harlots?' bid Perusim Shammai .
So's Simon say, 'Don' such got arts
What need be mastered
For a cunny be a pawky thing.
And dare I say Jesu be a'some hazard
And trepidation 'mongst these diners
For I see Matthew pluck our rebbi's purse clean
As his savior's plate.
So 'spect the bloke ta keep up wif broken pegs
But prove he straight away be a naughty geezer
And much ta our likin'.'
And what be a publican but ta squat a bit a'Tibi's trove,
What mean no harm ta the guineas.
And rape and plunder be as close to Aramaic
As these dago shites like ta utter.

And didn't Jesu imply that he be Jove

Ta these kitt's Kronos.
Anyways what part of ol' K. be left a'Pelasgi dissect.
          Our blubbery little lad
                    Ta atone that sin ta some feathery father
For disgraceful hole he squirt from.
                    None a'his makin' the paternal wad
                    What be Panteras the archer, liege a'Rome
                    And scourge a'me brethren.
This be inauspicious commence
                    Ta sovereign claims a'me rebbi.
               No doubt we got Jew Joves
          Right down the road in Zorah
What likes a'Samson slew the Philistines.
                    But I doubt our rebbi be another round,
Not a true Nazarite though his hair not be bobbed.
               But the lad bolt through the hoops a'many a'barrel
                    Ta make misery
Lookin' for the bottom a'the world.
And a couple a'John's boys, Tameo and Parthalan ,
                    Come ta the rebbi and ask
          "What we and the Perusi need starve,
                    While your lot glut and gorge?"
And Jesu say, "Can the weddin' guests mourn
          Long as the bridegroom be among 'em?"
"Depends on the bloody bridegroom," say our Tameo.
               "Toss that piss what married me sis, Berti, didn' I.
What the wanker fuck his mate's wife in the dunny
               On me lit'le Berti's weddin' day."
So's Jesu say, "The days will come, when the bridegroom is taken,
               And then they will fast."
"Doubt it, mate. For this fuckin' bridegroom I see before me
               Make a famine a the present
          Where plenty return at his remove.
And not no wineskin shite neither.
               Me bloody skin be as bantlin' as yours
But there be no bloody bloat ta it neither."

And back ta our nicks and shakes.
          Ain' I slip a fix a'datura on the ruler's daughter

What be hard run wif the rabble.
What Jesu come next day to raise among a tumult and laughter.
        And didn't the dose be spot on
As she on cue as though sleepin'--- wake.
            And a shill we grease what cries bleedin' from the twat
What no one a'the stench get close ta gander
            And the two Zebedee boys feign blindness
Bumpin' up on purses and keys and puttin' jacks
                On a long day a'hooks and alms, what that be.
And the boys declaim the rebbi
                    Wif bellow out a'they's soulful pulse,
        So smart and gorgeous, he name them the Boanerges
For the thunder what forecast such silver.

And Simon play a dumb demoniac
                    Yet be not a stretch for his flailin'.
        For our rebbi stride the stage a'Sepphoris
            And a such matters we abate a his judgment.
But Simon puff our wares, didn'he, flaggin' on wif
        "Never was none like this seen in Israel."
So the Perusi say, "He casts out demons
                What must palaver wif the prince a'darkness."
        What be some what many a'the rebbi's disciples suspect,
What don't know pulleys and beams be the logic a'his craft.
        The trepid he need most ta excuse
And danger at the hands a'those confused.
                For what be queue a'nails and cross,
Trickery or sorcery? But bofe be a guinea decree.

        So's our rebbi spread blame over many a'us what follow
Wif a bump in pay and a juke a'the bounty a'the tribe's trousers.
                And we be made twelve ---
    Judas and Kananaios, Thaddeus and James the Son of Alphaeus,
Rebbi's twin what be Tommy Didy
            And be rank nepotism if ya's ask me.
            But be I not one ta protest
                What be a gillie's death for sure,
For he be not the archangel and the rebbi be not god
                So why be this rebbi's breastplate

What take a fatal blow?
        The fuckin' dagos be a'demons certain that.
    And there be Philip, innocent a'any cause,
        And blank Bart, what ta be wif his mate,
Apostasize his potatos./potatoes.
And James and John Zebedee
What carry the rebbi's words upon their breaf
    As it be morrow's fish gut.
An' whose left?
        Oh yeah.
Simon and his bruvver Andrew,
     One's what got no salt in 'im
Even as his bruvver mark guinea and Herodian blood
        Wore crossed his apron like herring offal.
    And the rebbi warn, "Start slow. Go but to the sheep a'Israel.
And preach for five easy payments ta what be me father
      By measure a'the levy a'that guinea twat Tiberius,
What one be thy god
     And the other a Palatine cha-cha.
       For fuck me if the kingdom of heaven be not at hand.
And by such calculate they be marvined
     What by warrant they bellies be ta follow me
So that a crust under the snout
      'Pear a demon cast out.
You blokes be goin' as sheep 'mong the wolves
     Ta morph ta wolves among sheep.
Takes dem blows a'the flagella
       And dem what flogs ya in the synagogues
And drags ya before councils and courts
     For a brawl, or a spate a'sparrowin'.
      Be it murder or fraud,
For our crimes they will deliver us up
     For nothing turns bruvver against bruvver
      Than what we seek in his name.
And you will be reviled as what
      What we done will be revealed.
And be on the dodge lest ya not enjoy the fruits a our cheek
     And I be right behind on the lamb much as thems
What ain't been made.

Not but ta have ya be like me
But ta suss it for me own.
For ain't I on the spot? "
But we don't get guff
About this sparrow shite.
Acknowledge your bloody self.
What we be worth two or ten sparrows
And talk a'him invokin' his pa,
What will fuck us over if we don't mind.
For what be sparrows ta me but me callin'a pick pocket.
And his pa be Panteras, a bloody Roman git,
What sure be fuck us all and as well our rebbi
And do him first and last. So's I say, "Best
Cubby thy own bottom Jesu
Lest someone see source a true bread in your body
What be a few coins tweet 'bout yo' nest,
Ya ignorant shite. And don't be threatenin' us
Wif what be delivered past life be bore
For what nuffin' you here provide
Forecast a'nuffin' what you foretell."

So he be pissed, the scrawny fuckin' ratchet.
And yelp he, "Don't think I come ta bring peace a'earth."
And I "No mistake a'that, asshole.
What bloody botch we seen anon."
And again he "I ain't come ta bring peace but the sword.'
And I, "Blowhard! Fuck off! Where be this sword
But thy tunic be its proscenium
And Magdala's cunny its overture?
See thee a sword in your brethren's hands even as
It be dear Kananaios's blood surety?
And Iscariot be blood a'sicarii
But faint at sight a'korban
And leave off the most worthy morsel.
And didn't he grieve miserable at loss a'his dad."
For what pa or ma you earthly rift us from
'Cept most killed by the guineas
Be you what stand amongst us
Not ta be shoved aside and stuffed in a jar

What we might pickle your pimply ass."
And for dear departed mum and dad
                Me popped him a dry melt crossed his cheek
        What be dead if not by his hand
Certain his mouf'.
                        Ergo the bastard take a chuck at me
Finkin' he got a bit a'his ol' man in 'im.
                His dad be a'that dago lot.
            So I decked the bloke and boot him in the ribs,
And he smile up all toofs bleedin' at the gums
            And pass out what fall wif a puff a'dust
                What blow cradle that bugger
In a crown a'starry night.
                What we be shorn a'our kin
                    Ta him what kin not keep plain.
                What he havin' a mug?
Dad what we not see but this Roman git
A'the Judas/ Matthias riots
                When this Panteras porked his ma,
What abase ol' Joe suffer
                And what be Joe's bid a boy
                        What turn the other cheek
While his hand be found in any artless pocket.
                This be the sum a the bloke's sway and temper.
And Simon picked him up and brushed him off
                    For a buzz was needed and needed a'that
The same smug prick for many a'connie
                Want ta cut that pretty face,
And not but guinea alone but fellow Jew.

This pip be not a Maccabee
                What be wrought a'his sword
            But that daughter shank her mum.
Or son his dad
            And Pilato guffaw
At new delights a the circus
                And Syriaca prate a new Plautus or two.

            And give a cup I be sure.

But cup be but a pool a'bloody bile
       In his name what possess all the waters
Like some fuckin' kitt corpus Senatus.
        Him what prophet
Be righteous in his eyes alone,
        Blindfolded in this life
But to walk in light ta the next.
      And whats' ta say we get buggered a'life
In the next and the next and the next...
      What paskalakki our dear rebbi spew
And we be off what ta change masih's porkies inta cake
       What be bartered a'bread and wine
And bit a'bacon and sauce a'that.

And be this John wink or hoodwink,
      What many from their labors bathe yet
Shorn a funk be flushed again by the oracle
      What cause chafe in many and bitter palsy.
    For Jesu fear offense a'John
What got mouf enough ta piss off the Antipas
    Over a bit a'Herodian cooze.
      And rebbi raise him up a bit
   Above his hem, didn' he?
And chrism him prophet in his name
    What ta duck blood feud
Between two hot crews.
    And no Elijah be this John,
     What Jesu christen false
What forgive for sake a'bilks and gilts
    When a clarion a'his masih be his employ and concern.
Nor cult like the Nazarene
      What no twig so much as an adee-os ta mum and dad
    Lest his fish be cleansed a'Jesu's shite
     Wif muvverly daggle and a savory plate.
 Na more than what dear Elijah allot Elisha,
     So our rebbi be a haughty git
What be stuffed a'fetishes a'his truly.
    And them's what's got ears ta hear
Better they be cut off what not hear him, and him alone

That be the prophet pretty.
A glutton and a drunkard
What cavort wif publicans and talonas
Hung wif all baws and wit
What be a'the damned.
Drunk our rebbi and curse cities
What he not easy punk
Like they give a bloody fuckin' good goddamn
What see but the miracle a'their enslavement
By dago heathens what by nay deed, wit nor hygiene
Not like ta be a'any god's favor
Much less the presence ta stomp the chosen.
Better Sodom what not heard his pitch
Than Capernaum what not find the rebbi false
But for time and desire what hear his shite.
Bethsaida be hard under guinea caligae.
And he rib his daddy's works
They be a'infant squeaks and coos
What void a'Sodom be not worthy
While rebbi's purge be but a stinkweed reverie
Ta be visited upon the bohunks what follow him.

Yeah. And thanks, Pops, for bidin' us rude cherubs
Wif palaver your boy duff exclusive.
No matter it be clear Dionysi as Pilato be Pentheus.
Though 'pon good authority
What be ta Bustan, ta Cephas,
Ta Chasina, ta Heli, it be the procurator's piles
What grease our rebbi's flight ta Gehenna.
And a'that Thessalian cow what run Aegyptus
Be there Osiri born a'Isi once done up, rose a'his own.
So might not the wops be wise a'Magdala's flams
By the yaw and tow a'readin' books,
What we skints can't but have heard tell.
Who preach what his bruvver Didy bring back
What be about Indi,
Be called Isa Masih a'Bodhis and Devas,
And yoke a'his twin hand
While Yeshua take up arms a'Palmyra and

Ape Roscius at Sepph before Magdala
      Turned Didy's meanin' inta a pitch ta the yokels.
    Or Mifras what be a'blood rites and ritual meat.
What foster mithraeums.
      And what Roman soldiers and customs officials,
Like that jack batsi, Gatian, hold they's celestial butcherin'.

    And blank sky he entreat like its meat,
What we be but treated as swaddles in our nappies.
     Flesh a'him what can supply a few lumps
A'them victuals he moan about.
     And light be his burden last time
He sup first a'his own labors. For he says
    "Take me easy yoke," what, by fact, be true a'transom
      Port a'Skull Hill,
So we blokes come ta know what bait and switch be.
     Our hunger such ta gnaw pips and seeds
What these Perusim say we be filf before god,
     "What you blokes be about, be not lawful a'Shabbat."
    And masih mistake 'bout what be mind a'the priests
     And dither on about dirt holdin's,
What be discourse a'pinchin' another man's seed
    For be cuius est solum eius est usque
     Ad coelum et ad inferos, mind ya,
    Topos what 'sposed ta be purview a'our little genius.
But Jesu, prickly, sow discord 'mongst Hebrew grain
     Though land be a Samaritan
And fuckin' ain't I not be obliged to starve
    But bring a bit a'suffrage ta me belly for shite's sake.

And he present a palsy a'Simon
     Wif wand a'his hand ta cure,
    But the Perusim and Gentiles be cheesed off.
And he forthwith mingle among them, the Gents I mean,
    What our rebbi sought harb a'some future vig,
They be left ta collect a'their own peril.
     And a blind and dumb demoniac
   Be brought, what munnik be Beelzebub
    But we know it be our bruvver Tommie havin' a toss.

Not no Yeshua's twin
          As we confound the reader wif our dearth a'names.
Tommie be again cured as he be a ham
          What shimmies out a wrinkled palsy
And be a'the Aeolian graces as the bunko be buffed.
          And Yeshua be but ta gibe the Perusim
"Bout what he cast out a'his name,
          As he be not Satan
But what the pedi Greeks sight be a'the autocrat and
          What mysteries they not assent a'their's
Lest more honor be apprized reason
          As the hat return empty
And its brethren remain snug about the ears
          What better stir huzzahs 'bout such deeds.
And what be pardon a'god be exclusive
          Like our dago gov'nor Vitellius
So's ta be fear a'Roman pugio submit under Nazari law
          And feint the terror a'the people.

And what be true a'the fruit a'the tree
          Be true a'the market
For dun a repute affix the orchard a'its kulak.
          For what be a tree but it's clod
          And our rebbi bumpkin be all half-ripe words
What be not for fruit and bread but a load a'cobblers
          Such weakness be a'the whiny gillie.
Some's they like they's dry mount oysters do.
          But pray it first had they be but few.
And a drunk sowers insult many
          What good be ground hard and baked and
Hard bread thereof for guinea jowels. And thus by parable
          For what a stone mason know a'plantin'.

And don' our little Jesus be a bloody bounder
          When conjure this Jonah bloke,
          For a hole be a hole but also many a bloke's crib nowadays,
Where a fish's belly be ta drain a git's meat.
          And don't Jonah be such a gob.
          And to a snakefish be not a Jew a'peach pit

Or breed a'amanita
What ta torment the unclean in nature,
What our pilgrim be bum's rush a'his disposal?
What by example the clean not eat the unclean
That the unclean refrain from eatin' the clean.
A lesson swine and dagos be not gracious wif
But be equal ta the task a'eatin' each other
By each familiar turn.
And many the guinea gone missin' for passin' out in the swill pen,
Caligae 'et wif his tunic and pugio shat out,
Lest his ma lack token a'her boy's good character.
Or what heard by Fishgate that guineas roast a croc
But ta find a mate in the brute's belly
And what abide the mate a taste!

But how dotty be our rebbi
What claim greater juris a'Solomon
Heft what leave Sheba but a shadow a'Magda.
Warrant Magda be not wraith
But buck what throw these louts a fire.
And she have queenly affection to rule
What be sage enough make her ends line up
Wif the ends a'the earth.
Didy's grist and jist a wild Indi proverbs.
So two follies be one
That one imbue the other so to make a similitude a'nothin',
And a corona a'shame hard by torment.

His muvver and bruvvers once hail to stir him
Grow weary
For the unclean spirit be in him
And he account not their love
For they resist his pilfering and goad
What know by youth what be rank and false in the man.
For he be a'one father, one voice, mono y mano,
What other count three and the guinea archer
Be the fury for the third
What be debased by Rome's shadow
Yet a nang dilly a'the mind's vouch.

Sow? So what? Where be ground and where be rock
        Or birds or sun 'mongst thy hard scrabble words.
What be dust and what be furrow
          As hereby dust be a furrow and furrow a dust
As what famine a'the body mount that a'the soul.
      "This be but some such a Didy's rig babble," says I.
Ta better tip his course.
        But Jesu cry out, "Let 'em hear!?
          And I, "Oh, we hear aright little man."
For what git knows not his wife's furrow
       Impact a'what produce heirs,
But still cast a bit a'seed on the roadway.
         What wif a merchant be bereft a'his hearf
And cooze what god not nod as choice.
     Be it not nature you fuck with
       When nature attest full part and parcel?
A prime pump be keen.
    And make allowance if this be seed likes as ya mean.
      For back be keen to many mouths
And at first hairs we count, and keep our own
     Or by passion be owned a'others
But, by the by, a surly batch mean naught.
     And what seed be caste
       Be caste off the bones
    What not abide double naughts.
And this be me parable
     What grow fierce a'your bloody scoldin'.
And seeds here and seeds there
    When be not ten a'thousand
Don't know ta fuckin' farm
     And farm aright wifout your tauty almanac.
And here's your bloody muvver and your bruvvers
   What wait your honor.
So put down thy wine and
     And stand the fuck up,
And greet your kin as the law demands,
    Or catch a bloody whack."
And he be genial but clear his kin need not his words
    Nor merit thereof

Like they be bloody badu.

And what parables be way ta confound kitt law and Torah
    For what addle be in these riddles.
And what a magistrate intend be not what our rebbi lodge.
      Guinea logic mocked ta cut and frame all this sand, he say.
         His parables mean what ta the Perusim and that ta
Thursdays
     And render unta Caesar be but a bubble
       For what trouble the guineas serve.
What them parables be a bit barker and burlesque and encrypts
    What flower behind the ear a'what seeds he behold
What bear fruit in any batch or clump a daft bloke fancy
     For these be bearer a'no seeds but death and terror
For what man sow weeds but a'the mind
       So the belly be unresolved and the spirit broke
And wheat be burned as rags
     By those bound up by such fables.
And the rebbi hid everything in fictions as hedge against fidelity
    For why a universe what be ab ovo a bang a'some mustard seed
And forego a'its tree and branches,
      But what some tosser be Yeshua make a slight
A one hand what be sowers and reapers
     While the self-same be sown and reaped
What need a'our rebbi what ta burn what ignore him wif the chaff
     What for many generations bore fruit
And saw weed in those what would deny them.
      And what our Yeshua pull from his ass
Keep therein windy a prolix as blather and blethers
     What keep a mind from man and god
Much less his stores.
For what but by lottery be found in the furrows
      As lot a many be ta starve by and by
Awaitin' their pearl, what our rebbi say be easy and common
      For the rare and valuable be but his lure and woo
But ta my mind his be
     What covet pearls be cast from the net
Like a shell a'it's tref shucked.
And be we off ta his tango

Where abide his blood.
And he be at temple what his bruvver James toss
      "What sack! Pitching his shite in synagogue
      What every cod and cunt knew
          He was a part time board banger
Makin' the shice up as he be goin'."
      And Maryam slap Jimmy upside his cronum
For she be at much despair a Yezhua's babble
      Wif such good and learned about.
What be blamed a bastard a'his kitt daddy, poor soak.
      And what Yeshua muddle
Too may at Temple know and he be caste out
      And but for deference to his ma
      And threat the key a'the city be but a'the stocks.
And pray Yeshua be not shunted to Pilato,
      The bloody Roman fuck so despised
A bit a'blasphemy be disposed a'what walk among 'em,
      So the citizen wade not waist deep in errant blood
And the muck slow the advance a'the true Messiah.
      Tall tales as what spill from Macheras
Where Antipas supposed ta
Behead the Baptizer for fear of his legion and
Oath ta the daughter a'Herodias
      Without comportment of a dago writ,
What would see Herod's nog posted below John's
As be some bloody kabob
      Wif all us fine Jews what piss off Tibi and Pilato.
These be the stakes me shite born Nazarene
      Not what eels and bread
What thy truck from elder Zebeddee,
Me and Ibraham like Samson ta stone be our shoulder ta wheel.
      But the crowd not gulled by the eels
Or Yeshua's clabbered t'oughts, such tref be left a'the gulls
      As what be gulled.
And carp what feed upon orts and shites tref be Jonah's sign
      As our rebbi carp upon such sweepings.
And put our hunger on the Perusim and Seduqim
      What fasted twice whilst our fast be willy-nilly ta starve
Or speak not from hunger

Lest in mid-plaint we trifle a fucking sign.
Such that Simon succumb wifout so much as a nib
  What all look as any day and Yeshua as any man
    And thus the daft Ben Jona be first inverse a sense
And likes ta die thereof if the sound and fury got a say in it.

And Judas ta coax his rebbi ta take upon the boat a'Zebedee
  The crowd restive a'the tref and stale bread
And the rebbis fatal and witless buggings what see no sign on earth
  But to be a sign in heaven.
And for fear a'the mob Simon and the boanerges be off a'the skiff
  And the rebbi ta some solitude.
And Judas behind wif the rebbi say,
  "The boy ain't et awl day," ta Andrew.
And Andrew "What be a'that man's particulars escape me.
  You may be his love scabbard
But I not part my ways a'his means.
    And thus he be flush wif me."
"What he lo! Missing Zebedee's skiff
  Yeshua be upon the jetty,"
    Pellicled at high tide what 'pear he stand upon water
At what we laugh and John taunt, "What rebbi? Be thy at miracles
  When no tithe be advanced.
Waste ye that ye not want, little man."
    But fretting Yeshua catch a slip and fall in
  What Simon the Whale scoop up our bit a'leaky Jonah
And put him skinny proper in the skiff,
  For certain Yeshua be an ass.
But, ass or no, he not drown on our watch
  Lest we retreat a'our former labors.
  And chill and fever overtook our little rebbi
Such that he imagined some Perusim and Seduqin
  Truck about ta see him.
And he reamed their word even ta disregard his own.
  And likewise a fever be crowds
What not there lest they be befuddled by such enigmas.
  And young John grow uneasy and cruel,
"Say you not what goes into the mouf defiles a man,

But what comes out the mouf, this defiles the man.
What useless riddles for doth not my cock
Both access and egress your mouf
          As does Magdala's cunnie
               But to be no defile hither or fro?
Does not the rank flesh a swine and fetid heat
          Slay more fuckin' guineas than our swords
               Much less your bloody puzzles?
There are no blind men here lest it be us?
               So for once, just shut the fuck up!"
          And our rebbi be calmed and smile
For there be a bit a'father's care in our towheaded boanerges
     What Yeshua's daddy Pantera not deploy
               And what be that someday mark the end a'the world
For son's hatred a'the father.

And first off upon his resurrect from fever
               We venture ta kill a little girl,
          Daughter a Canaanite woman Danya.
Her child we urged ta waft mad
          And be subsequent cured a'the rebbi
               Before we spare a bit a'bread and broth.
And the tiny waif die from exertion
               So that demons appeared cast out.
                    And that be it and no more
As our cruelty now be beyond ignominy.
               What our rebbi proscribe what be just
What many now knew he be wrong.

And such be our rebbi come unto Caesaria Philippii
          A low and vile mind he be fixin' ta die.
And rebuke Simon ta be a dunce what protest
               His gloomy denoue
As to call his savior Satan and halt,
          The fuckin' masih not a moon from drownin',
His mind a tatter as he be snarled a contendin' demons
               What but fiat we attest he be son a'the livin' lord
Ta settle his spirit what some see as a cryin' babe
               Ta be put ta sword

What give out concealment ta the enemy
        That blood be spared.
And tell no one he be the anointed
    As John tell there be a danger a'that 'malfunction'.
What we roll about quoitin' our bellies
        What the lad's proper object be 'malefaction'
    Though his abuse do be a bit canny.
And our rebbi say "Who do men say that the Son of man is?'
Look. I not say they be not riddles.
    Nor not riddles what the riddler be aim or butt.
But these our Yeshua's we sick with knowledge of such that
      Andrew flings his arms in the air
And sighs and paces and Matthew shout "Aw! Jimmy Britts."
   And Yeshu come again,
    "Who DO men credit the Son a'man be?"
And a proper soggy, Simon, as he be a tutor a'books,
   "Oh! Oh! I know! I know dis!"
As all we do. But he ta butter the bottom a our bit a'masih
   What get turned about for our rebbi
Be a late a right moody geezer.
   What you say up, he say down.
    What you say light, he say dark.
What you say life, and he say deaf.
   And Yeshuah he be 'bout ta die. What Simon
Be but a pup what ken his bit a'biscuit
    Lord forbid, this be not true.
What the rebbi shout "Get behind me Satan."
   And the fat man lurch and fall upon the ground.
And grumble 'bout me ear days out,
    "What I be hindrance, what save his skinny ass.
This be me thanks as but charity be in me."
   And I, "As we be his household
What follow him ta the mausoleum
   "Though we be sound a'limb
And of reasoned heart. What be this deny oneself.
    Perjure thy being
   And take up the cross
But ta follow swine ta the slaughter pens.
    But ta abort ourselves like we be but the rebbi's suttee

And by what our guinea masters do flourish.
       We be forgot as be but a cult felon-de-se.
     For what be asked but we be topped a'our own ambition.
       Our own appetites.
     For what profit be in forfeit.
And what life be well-negotiated wif concealment
     On word a'this donkey's anus, Jesus.
Sure and be I one what not taste deaf
      'Til I taste a'our daft rebbi's kingdom
And then me belief whistle hosannas ta me kismet."

Ovverwise whosoever lose his life for his sake be findin' it.
     But, no doubt, at Yeshua's dispose
As he smack a'all illusion. And wif henbane and datura
     From me stash,
      Simon and Yeshua be off wif the boanerges
Ta Gamala. What I suspect ta get blazed and poo stab young John
     What time honored youth be fancied in its turn
And smoke be gateway a'many pleasures and easings.
      And don't light and white garments be reported.
And Moses and Elijah as to attest a gnarl bit bite a bane
     What bring John and James ta watery squats
Doubled upon the ground
     They heard not the rambling hallucinations.
A the prophets and thus be grateful for Yeshua what say
     Tell no one a'the vision
Til the son a'man be raised a'the dead.
     For neither the boys nor Simon know
What the fuck was said by them ghosts
     And didn't fancy their little rebbi
     Havin' a second stab at life's breaf ta grill 'em.

But a sober Yeshua don' practice what he preach
     And breaks covenant that the Baptist be Elijah,
    What make the Baptist eschaton
And terrorize all about a'the unholy day
     When they will no longer abide a their fields and flocks
But be tossed a'the whims a'the cosmos.

But be where our bloody git break it off
As it be but a bit a'idle chatter.
        And we be off what ta fix this boy
                What cure be coin.
But fits as farce,
            But ta give the rebbi gall ta wring out a tithe
For the pissant whine 'how long he bear us'
                As all he bear far as I see
                Be his scrotum and his purse
By what intent a'which bofe dangle
                A full view a'those with eyes ta see.
        But the crowd naught but a boy Yeshi turned back
From the contort of a landed eel what some demon be fled.
            And again wif the morose shite
Be he heavy 'bout his gaffs
        As he plant coin ta seed his Maggie's naked swell.

Once men be bound in fish
        Where now but a shekel be found
                    And that orphan copper bound a tax
        Before a cold mug or a bit a'ackawi and figs.
God what shrink fish ta comport wif men's hearts.
        As be Yeshua's arts what he be killed
            Simon and the boanerges ta spirit the body away.
Didy say what be his twin
        What Yeshua pine for his chicken Aamir
                What a week we lost our wee masih fuck
                    Ta the arts a'pedi bung.
And so all howl and horror
                Hither he grab another by Capernaum
        But fear we censure what protest much a'his aim
            And be all out our coppers and kippers.
                What we be like whelps?
What I take ta be ta fornicate' what he pine his twink.
        And soon I'll wager be wantin' Simon ta shave his ass.
        And his back. And Yeshi contorted wif temptation
For this be pretty little tow head.
            But he just can't knick the boy
And creep be what call him his mate

As he what fuck many a spink
Be sudden franked a child.
                    And what be humble a child
As brash be our rebbi when but a bitty wank.
                    And what I want wif a boy be it Yeshua
Wif Aamir slung over his chest.
            As some warnin's ta his priests what we resent
As it be filfy habits he take from Moses
                    As he the Hellenes a'Tzippori
            What be no clear proscription a'the law.
But terror a'the wee lad's ma
        What see Yeshi wif a wild grief flinging about
Talkin' a'pluckin' at his eyes
                        And starin' upon his raised hands
Like they's cudgels but ta strike the child's bosom.
        And he cry, "See you not despise these little ones."
At which breach I snatch the little wanker
                        And pass him off ta his ma.
                    And yet the rebbi rant on 'bout some airy flock
Weepin' a shepherd risk a hundred ta find one,
            What turn the crowd a'such addle
What I'll wager graze their share a'jumbuck
                        Delivered as it be a no proper sage.
  And the boy delivered from the hand a'our crazed rebbi.
And Yeshi conclude between he and his abba
            What might be a torment
As his daddy Pantera soon cut his froat as coddle his bung.

            And what it be he not trust us
And he curse the tax man as a Gentile
            What Matthew mock and tease
Til Yeshi convulse with grief and frof
    As ta us bear witness he be not a tax upon his brevren
And John and Jude be quick ta temper his mood,
            Strokin' gentle his nape and callin' him lord.
And he gazed up at them pitiably,
            Full sweet and a much oblige.
And Didy step forth not three years return
            A slave ta Abbanes,

Sold by his twin Yeshi
What want show Maggie a good time.
What Didy's life be spared
A bit a'fortune if ya's askin'
What his forbear be poor Uriah
But what put Yeshi a spec a'King David
What yarn much weigh upon the boy.
And at Tzippori didn' he play at this Stultus Matellus
A mock tragedium a'Lucilius
What bloke be cuckolded by Jove,
Shipped ta the front by Menelaus
What want a piece a'his missus
What take sloppy seconds be it aft a'god,
And the luckless hubby cut ta ribbons
At the battle a'Panoply
So what Yeshi say "if your bruvver sin against you,
Go and tell his fault,"
Ring out a slight in Didy what wander Indi in chains
A'what his punk bruvver covet.
"Keep your tongue in your cheek
As it be ta save your prick and keep it to its tunic.
You'll not hear me, witnesses or no,
Be your head stuffed with the ardor a'demons.
Be you ta me worse than a goyim or the tax man
And I make no apology for Matthew or Zacchaeus.
And don' promise me heaven
As heaven waft betwixt Maggie's thighs.
And what gather twos and threes in thy name,
Be thou butchered like a dago king
And god be on thy breath as Brut,
So rank thee be."
And Simon step between the binate
For sake a'blows and ask,
"Rebbi. Be I forgive me bruvver seven times?"
And Yeshua what fear a bruvver's beatin' say
"Nay but seventy times seven,"
What number but barely acquit transgresses upon Didy.
And what ta save his skin pitch tripe a'servants
And masters, and what forgivin' debt

What make Didy both master and slave,
    What lost love a'homeland, and family and Maggie
For Yeshua be not a'these, but be 'bout money.
    What in our confusion forgive
But not forget our rebbi's lies for if the prize be a kingdom,
    A false teacher be valued more than true.

And the Perusim ask "As you say rebbi.
    What god join, be no man what put it asunder.
      But if not Moshe from whence we hear his word
    What tell put thy wife away."
And Yeshua, grip his head as upon a vice and moan
    "With what trick do you confound me.
Demons, be thee make a fool of me favver?"
    "Mais non. None but Gamaliel make a fool a'you.
    And I but a boy. Our father be praised.
For be thee more than Moshe
    What lead his pikey band 'bout Judea three years.
And don't your wife get a little on the side
    What say you be grounds."
And dazed Yeshua babble about three eunuchs.
    But be quite not forfright 'bout the fourf.
But not the disciples or the Perusim
    Laugh at this pitiable man
      But show mercy upon his dead eyes.
And nippers and sprogs be curious
    Press upon the pikey loon,
      What tears become cackles
And trepidate Simon and James and meself.
    And at his grasp the children whoop and bale.
And Yeshi stagger about what seek alms of accord,
    A blessin' his nog be aright
What wif scuttled Moshe,
    Yeshi block a dandy what afright say he be wifout sin.
"And thee be perfect give all ta these,"
    What be Simon and James
    And we take our solace, rebbi be back in sense.

Refreshed a fits he speak a'camels and ropes,

What negotiate the eye of a needle,
I hear be a hole in the east wall a'Damascus
What camels direct a'Parthia and other hostiles,
As be Asinai and Anilai, Be unloaded,
Checked for arms and pass upon their knees,
Grovelin' ta that bloody fuck Tiberius.
But Matthew counter our rebbi be not so daft
Try but a rope ta a needle and this be a easy concern
What any bloke take up a hem.
Smaller than a camel's ass and sharper than a blade
What we can bring ta a shakedown
For rich fucks be coy what got meat
And that meat be passage
A good favor a'any man's god
Is the way them cocksuckers read it.
But may thee one day be fitted for me garotte
Or a rope coiled down ta a noose's eye.
And Jude quip Simon be plain sight fat as a camel's hump
Assuaged a'Gihon,
He what find heaven at the bottom of a stew pot.
"Aye," be wot a Bart. "Toss that dog a bone
And this dog do wifout,
Such be his franchise on charity."
And Simon Peter draw his bonin' knife,
What Yeshi stay, "Stink, Stink.
Caul thy blade." He bein' a bit've a blodger and fat so.
What we all be true and honest call him Stink.
And again Yeshi say our crust be in heaven.
A good distance that.
Yet what many ta finish be ta fall on their swords
And strike for straightaway.

"Be there lot's to jump the queue" asked John.
What Yeshi babble some parable
What pay out a life a labor wif less reward than
Indolence and indifference toward god.
And that be his fields be his the laborer's blood
And these be but chattel.
What many a'the crowd turn ta Barabbas

And the Gamalas what promise land for blood
Not fill the guinea aqueducts wif Jew sweat and tears.
　And thus with a word many a gangster be made first.
　　And many a bunko last.

What Maggie return from preachment at Hebron wif
　　Salome Z., Seraphia and Johanna Chusa.
And they be with a bit a coin.
　　　And they's be mutton and wine about,
　And smokes what extol our res gestae
　　Timely for Judas' patrimony be squandered
　And he despair a burying his dear ol' dad.
And Maggie say straight away they make for Jerusalem,
　　Where Yeshi warn a'the twelve one be set upon
By the chief priests and scribes
　What be proscribe a guinea law to sentence death,
　　　Send him up ta the kitt speculatores
What by Rome's law bear writs a'execution
　　　And by hanging itself all Jews be proscribed.
　　And Yeshi claim it come a omen
　　What he loaf at Camel's Hump.
And they whisper anon it be Jude spoke
　　　Upon occasion as Thaddeus
　What be lamb a'Passover and ta what purpose,
Though Maggie be a menace in her temper.
　　　And none sure a rebbi's decretum
That the bloke so abused be rose a'the third day
　But perhaps his bits and parts be stuffed in a hole
And a crowd roused a innocent blood
　What be not a portion a'this dago ruin.
And Salome what mid-wife Yeshi and Didy
　Approach Maggie and the rebbi
　That they not be chose for double cross ta the kitts
And didn't she slough Yeshi and Didy upon the world,
　　Up ta her elbows in their ma's quim.
　And Maggie and Yeshi nod yes
　　For what be ta lie a'that transit
　Even though the twins be so disposed.
And did they not eat her bread as old Zebedee

Sparged the wheat a'his sweat.
And she and the boys sacrifice everything
    For this low pikey quest
            Want cant more ta cede .
        See they not fit ta give her pups a bump,
That be James and John.
            And at rebbi's right and left will do.
What ovvers claim head and feet, ass and prick.
        And Andreas perch the masih's lap
            And fat Simon mount his bony livery
    What miracle be a wont acquit that cross.
What all aboard likes they be acrobats
            A'the circus a'Tzippori or Caersaria.
        What ta break our frail rebbi
What at best sit a wraith on a stick.
        And Maggie tumble down,
            Tears a laughter soppin' her cheeks
Feet in the air and belly braced.
    And be so Chusa and Seraphia what esteem a good jape.
But Jesus wheeze out "whoever would be great among you
        Must be your servant first,"
What the disciples dismount and recoil at the rebbi's recount
            Of promotes what be bondage.

And what wanks make a this but Yeshi be 'bout expiry
        Wif stink on his shoulders and alarm a slave's consequence.
And we went out Jericho there be two blind men,
            What told a'who's passin' cried, "Fuck you Jesu.
 Son a'David, ya scabie bum."
    What be wif them the leper Sanballat
                What not be cured a'him
            And dwell amongst many what be so dispose.
"If I be thee I'd sod off, ya pig's ass,
        Before I patify Ham be your tribe
            And curse you thus
        And arrive me crutch about thy head wif blows."
And Yeshi, "Must your soul rot too that you harbor such evil.
        Go to the water wif this one what bathe thee,"
And Jude be ginger 'bout the leper

What cast off his crutch and cry
"I not be washed a'thee what extort for gifts.
I be shed a'thee what soon be hanged
And thy scrubber wif ya, ya daisy prick."
And so mocked wif words we be scorned wif stones.

And straightway we retreat a'this lunatic
And the rebbi summon me and Bart
Ta go inta town and pinch a couple a'asses
What we be clear these be a'four legs
For for doin' the ass a'two legs be but us.
At what we balk as we be thereby horse thieves
And be it not Thaddeus ta be gived up as the lamb.
But Yeshi say tell 'em "Thy Lord hath need a'them."
And Barty cite, "Oh that be ducky, ya daft mug.
Best speech a bit whilst we dive the crowd.
And by what crown we got acquire the mounts."
What our rebbi declare some sir be the daughter a'Zion,
What put in mind Seraphia and Johanna already boost said asses
And the "Thy Lord… shite" be a code
And we but transport the contraband,
What still get a yardie hanged.
So's we brought the asses to him
And the crowd spat in his path
Such that Simon Peter slipped and risin' cursed the jeerin' mob
What mocked and laughed "Hosannah ta the son a'David."
What Yeshi turned the crowd wif a fox's rashness
Overturn the counters a'the temple brokers
And in the melee be beggars blind and lame,
And cullers and traders,
And we scooped to our folds gold mugshots a'the guinea king
And make our way under the walls a'the Antonia
What way be greased wif a bit a'tribute for Tibi's fightin' man.
And the blind and lame were well-stood by our rebbi
And sang conviction 'Hosanna ta the son a'David'
What can trickle a bit a'coin and transmute a spot a'bread.
But we made haste ta Bethany
Passing close Sanballat's hole.

And our rebbi bloody pissed a'the transpire the day before,
      Has a slash the base of a knobby ficus.
And he find naught fruit ta fondle
         But his own plums and the nutter curse the tree,
And claim ta me and Jimmy he done it in
        Wif a bit a'Mickey Bliss
When clear that arbor be dead some time.
And he "If ye follow me blind…"
And what say Jimmy "Get woke up ta gaze upon a gallows.
Go ta sleep Yeshi as there be
Where thy sense be a best regard,
In dreams and tyro fantasy.
      Curse thee a tree?
And heed what curse thee."
And Yeshi think ta forestall the priests and elders
      But few hold John a prophet
        Proved how easily rebbi be scorned
And not commit a'his abba but hold his tongue.
      And what tax collectors and harlots
As be Perea still rife wif bof commerce
      And but a handful a'hoes in our ranks
What we repeat upon them as they be goomah.
And Matthew a tax man be by fine line a felon.
      And what make a his fable
What some boy be a harlot a'his vineyard.
      Such be this stupid man.

But he kept a shuck about some fool wif a winepress
      What goof all but abandon pressin' wine
But who be about feckless murder
      When drink be at hand
And who put evil before drink
      What more like ta be after
    What all Yeshi's palaver 'bout John's head confirm
      For drunk the Antipas broach Roman writ.
So's I says rebbi "Let's not asperse our wineries
      Wif rabble of amok vintners
What murder their betters."
      And so he be off another a'his barmy tales

'Bout a king what set a posh table
          What his business connects make light.
What sense be a'this as me own bowels
          Wring out the last a'yesterday's dolma.
And what be the nature a'this king
          That his guests make no marriage but kill his servants
              But ta avenge as this king be a bloody bastard
That give some offense and what burn the homes
          A'those what turn away.
And the food what rot durin' the razin'
          Be fed ta those what clearly make the king kak
This be our rebbi desperate his due
      Yet suffers one be cast out for lack of a weddin' garment
              What oblige the king ta supply
When a multitude lie mangled and burned
          And terror of the rag pickers at his table
Lest he immolate them for what be whim or wot insolence.
And Yeshi confound John wif friend and he the groom,
What he a many a'his fables be the bride
      And what the baptized be the bride
              Or ponderable patch thereof
While I be tid a'hunger and addled prattle
          Til I be done in a'this lit'le man and his baffled amblings.

Yet Yeshi kibitz wif the Perusim about the dago tax
          What be render unto Caesar what be that shit Caesar's
And god's what be god's.
Ta what Gamaliel ask what say ye
              When Tibi would have what god have too
      So he be such as god,
The Perusim clear of wit.
          Nor match for the Seduqim for not Abraham,
Isaac nor Jacob be no longer counted among the living
          Whom still require their wives account
Lest their fields be forfeit and their crops lie fallow.
      And what ease ta love a god what fright a guinea pilums,
Or neighbors what cowardly despair
          As we despise our neighbor as we despise ourself
What not die like Barabbas throwing off these Roman shits.

And what Lord say that Lord,
Sit at me right, till I put thy enemies under thy feet
        Wif not but a pruned pennywhistle beneath his cloak
        And a neck's be under Pilato's boot?
And left wif such tripe, none bother to cross examine,
        For what ask of a stone be a stone's.

And Yeshi be spoilin' for a barney
            For he be a qaurrelsome lit'le banty,
Either naff or wank.
        So sop the Perisum and the Seduqim before his people
But to slam their better natures wif weakness god's labor affords
        And wif dis one father but dis father be mute, or nod.
Or dead . But what his flesh be off ta Bingium.
                And for instruct we be wantin' since Moshe.
        But he woe, woe, woe the Perusim
        For what he himself seeks
And call them hypocrites what be his very enterprise
        For what altar be not a blood oath,
And what oath leave not a stained garment
        And what high and mighty Yeshi swear
He better be above it lest he be upon Tibi's altar
        Or some guinea legion's mifra,
        Or mere what bit a Magdala's goat he garnish.
What our rebbi would tithe justice and mercy
        As he learned ta tithe love a'Magdala
For no matter how much Yeshi rub the outside
        Be the inside a'the cup where the coin do clink
Then he slander the bones a'me abba
        As we be ta honor his though
            That bloody shite be a guinea archer.
And the people be pissed as they be reproved a'the prophets
        What not trace the prophecies nor regard their labors
Under this fuckin' dago king Tiberius.
So they pleased not see Yeshi again or his likes
And he wish them ill, screaming oaths and curses.
        And he curse Jerusalem
What many a'kitt procurator be at haste to fill

> But hedge his portend a'some shadowy and many ills
For he pull them from a dark garden
What we livin' call his culo.
And it be Yeshi's ass certain what be first front a'final days.
> Ta what he portend Magdala's treachery
For the madame snore and dish in her sleep.

And what be ta invoke Daniel by this bitter lit'le man
> What exhort flame and flood upon all manner a'thing
Many fear the hell he make inchoate wif fable.
> What be Daniel's prophecy
> Ta what our rebbi squawk all will be made clear
What we aright come ta fear and doubt.
> And what oppress mothers wif a winter route or Shabbat
But be stock and trade a'our guinea Caesar.
> And what be this ta the mountains
Or cling ta the rooftop but this land be parched
> What flood Yahweh proscribe.
And false Christs be that not he
> As surely Magdala set up Didy as bogey.
And don't eagles what gather be but called vultures
> Their society a gatherin' what rejoice at carrion's favor,
And the eagle be the dago standard what take its meat wet.

At once he curse the world ta twice spell it wif consolation,
> That he not know his own mind nor the vox populi
What would will a king ta strike their kitt masters
> For these be not the days of Noah
But the flood of Palatine vermin be upon us.
> And who be taken and who be left
Be writ if Tibi's speculatores
> That our Yeshi be struck dumb as he be deaf and blind.
> But his masih be as a fief in the night
What sure be hanged for not a fief be welcome,
> Special not no Jew fief before a world class dago one
But that Herodian be kitt vassal.
> Or be it a wise servant what prepares the master's food
What be held up trading rags and plumbago in Caesaria
Such that his stores be wasted.

And simple, bitter Yeshi see be but two ways ta squander
       And none ta husband and concord,
Or that we all be servants ta his fancy.

And so more fables as an ox might grunt to an ox,
       And what a brute's hind quarters shed more purpose
And abet more wisdom than these ten maidens
       And they's bloody lamps,
What be some wif oil and some lack.
       And be our rebbi ten bridegrooms
What be a godhead but three
    That his prick be well oiled
       And multiply like loaves where there be
    The stink a'fish.
And what merchant bear a knock in the night
       Sell a spot ta flighty girls.
Or parable what servants truck wif money changers
       What our lit'le goose lick masih drub in the temple.
And damn the cockney slave what fear the master's hegemon
       What be as imperial and bloody as the dagos.
And praise the shits what fiat be coin.
       And best be in darkness than light a'this wick.
He be off about sheep what be led ta slaughter
       What be meat, and blood for drink, and wool for rig
         As be they promissory.
And this king what be him be an abomination
What seek largesse a sheep behind prison walls.
And goats be what the fuck. Not it be for our meat and milk
       But that we not be puffters nor a cowardly disposition,
         You abandon us
What tongue be of a sheep what you say be a godly tongue
    So be not goat's among the righteous?
For his fucking worthies not reckon our masih
       But the least among what share
    No attributes a'this haughty prick
What be about judge a'any and know none
As they what choose not ta know him
And ta be left in peace.

Kayafa and the elders be a'their priestly duties
        While Pilato from Caesaria
                Wif his Tenth Fretensis and 12th Fulminata
What by bloody tutelage keep Jerusalem's Pesakh at peace
Even as the journey fire up the procurator's piles.
But what pilgrim care ta privy some rich dago's roids.
        And what dago king so heaped a'other men's treasures
        See a dead pharaoh and bloated minions
In the eye a'his subjects what Kayafa and the priests petition
        That be the rite and the act
                And know nothing a'Yeshi.
And we sojourn a'Simon the Leper,
        A scabie what Jesus not heal
As fraud be exposed. And a woman garnish rebi wif oil
As he be a goose and we be reproved
Because he die wif this stink on
                What could'a fed us a fortnight
If Stink and the Zebedees make their own repast.
And she be a memory for me toddles on Yeshi's say so
        And if me memory serve he fate the poor be always
        Even if him naught
As they be one a his credo's abidin' condiitons
        But me hunger be a condition wif a membrance too.

And one Nicodemus, a'Perusi, let four rooms a'the Golden Fornix
That his cult might gather. One be for Yeshi and the twelve.
Two for disciples not of the inner circle where I take me repast.
And a fourf for the ladies.
And rumor a'treachery spread frough the rooms
        For it be thought Magdala make
A mifra that night a'Thaddeus
Ta stir the rabble under Yeshi's topper.
But what smell a rat, it not be named.
Nor be it custom among these
                As all become heady and desolate wif wine
                And wif the cutthroat guinea, Atilius, lurkin' about.
Magdala resolute in the yard wif two asses,
        What ta be returned before sundown

Lest their owner post lien what be precipitate against her plan.
      She stomp and damn me nephew Shalmai
Be done a'her.
And Heli take ta his quarters lest the guineas be ta sport off this lot
      What I be in and about.
Why not I be spared the bloody, tripey mifra a'the rebbi
      As be all in the outer rooms
And thus there some faith be preserved.
      A blood julep be what Philly and I cede
And loath ta take the chalice but whiff
      What be ta my snout wine still.
And the bread be easy ta circumstance
      Lest there be some imponderable maggot,
      Yet the whole leave a bad taste in me mouf
What best be cleansed wif booze
      And a turn a bit a'stinkweed and rue.

And some turn from the rebbi
      What the bloody mifra be the spent a'their will
As it be the mest curd a'Osiri or
      The huddle and brood a'dago topkicks
      Nor likes to alight much coin.
And by such metousi Yeshi grip be loosed
      And what pissed get pissed by a dewy rue
What set ta revel at Gethsemane wif his twink Aamir.
      He among laugh and dance and fuck on the cool ground
And anoint many a bung what the rouse the neighbors
      And the guinea guard be called
What be led a'that fuck Atilius
      Command a'Gallus,
What spot Yeshi be a banty a'Pantera
      Same what throttle a lion in Sinai.
And take the rebbi what he lance this boil
      What repute put Pantera a mind a'the procurator
What be fuckin' trouble cocked inta existence.
      And Magdala counter Tad for guinea sport
And Judas heartreft kiss Yeshi upon his lips

And thus culled by the dagos come to naught for reckoning.
And Aamir from terror fled, be he but a child.
                And Stink rash to stay the dagos
Cut a temple servant about the ear.
And Tad, plump and flush, be wedged in a ditch
                Like a yam the earth will not loose
Nor able Matty and Magdala.
                So's appears Magdala whisper a bit ta Yeshua
What the guineas seize ta please Pantera
                As his bastards fair a'threat ta empire
What in kind be a threat ta daddy
                As the procurator not get buzz
                From some legionnaire what aspire ta optio.

And the guineas what be in search a bit a'revels a'their own
                Drag our rebbi ta the temple.
But Kayafa be lost in Pesach ta such dago nonsense
    What not grasp the import
                Much less the boding menace a the day.
Stung ta be so ignored our stupid Yeshi be "I query the Sediqui
                If they not be so disposed a'Pesach.
But says I "Best keep thy bloody mouf shut.
And now ta know for we come upon Pilato
                What wake ta his morning ablutions
And be want straightaway his fortune teller read his stool.
Best thou not mix in it,
For death be the rag what mops that man's ass clean."
                And didn't the guineas straightway hang Judas
    From an olive tree
For hangin' 'bout the neck a'Yeshi weeping
And detainin' the procession"
Here let me loose this yoke a'love, Yeshi," so this dago Carl
    What but cut the disciple from his object
And placed the rope.
                And seeing Judas so rudely disposed
Yeshi still not be shut the fuck up before Pilato
                What indisposed wif bad omens read a'blood in his stool,
Ass barnacles what dismissed Yeshi to the guard
                And disposed a'one, this masih Barabbas in his foyer

And what Jew did not know Pilato
        Be not about ta release the soul of an insurrection
            Back inta its corpus.
So Barabbas bloodied by many blades be tossed in a gutter,
The guinea detail quick ta turn to their rashers
            What get cold in the bowels a the Antonia.
And Yeshi others beat
            For he be an evil twaddler
And ill dispose Pilato what that very morning shit ill fortune
            A'this fool's coming.
So Yeshi be hanged not Thaddeus
                Who unbeknownst be named cause and sacrifice.
        And poor Judas besides
What be turned away sodden for Yeshi's twink, Aamir.
        And some rube from Cyrene be conscripted
To carry Yeshi's cross, the rebbi being bereft a'magic
Wifout me potions.
And I straightway borrow the pilgrim's kindlin'
        As that day keepin' mum and warm
            Be the breadth a that day's swot.
And out cry Yeshi "E'lo-I, E'lo-I, la'ma sabach-thani?"
What some hear "He call Elijah,"
    And others say be nonsense
        A'them desperate a'their fate
What follow this dunce,
                For it be clear Eloi.
    And a guard be set about Yeshi's tomb
        What the dagos suspect some fraud
For Magdala's words be a'the effect a'one a'theirs
        What be slain by the guinea
Rise after three days as what be asleep
        And a body snatch soon be rife wif rumor.
But I got no rue what bring back Yesh
        So's Magdala and Matthew kill the guard and
Loose the corpse wif Peter Fishstink, the Zebedees
        And a bit a'Johnny Gamala's crew.
        And Magdala fraud Mary and Salome
            What find the tomb empty
        But for Aamir what say Yeshi be risen

And what hysteric these good ladies be.
And Yeshi's twin Didy appear
And gather the disciples upon Tabor Hill
Where it rain and be cold and there be much complaint
          Among the brethren
And where their labors die.

PART V: The Grammys

So much beauty is wanton.
So much 'greatness' is suspect.
So much beauty is craven.
So much harmony suspect;
    Those verdant hills are abandoned corpses,
      So grievously affirmed
   That music should be the howling from hell
     If to live is to know the world at all.
What measure but time.
But now that time has been deposed,
The future's blood is thick upon the altar.
Base Golgotha's mop the sticky, damp floor
While tears of the old god's sing plainly
   To the few not writhing to gently weeping chords.
If the king does not pluck out his eyeballs,
THERE IS NO TRAGEDY.
Where the wealthy are not brought low
     For their crimes and calumnies
There is no justice.
Where the villain does not suffer denouement at his own hands,
There is no salvation.
Where the diaspora abandons a potter's field
    Of torn tickets, beer cans, condoms and candy wrappers,
There is no victory.
Where the chorus of the masses from the tympanum
     Whimpers in relief for some foreign other
They know not, there is no pathos.
They are paid to weep,
The scores of Carian women set apart in glittering gowns,
Practitioners of a corporate mourners' art.
   Death the perfect trope to romance sounds.
And permanence unlike its rituals cannot be feigned.
Lest the assembly line not be maintained.
And when they die there is no tragedy.
For what demise could lie in shit
So balefully self-congratulatory.

The best flawed just as us all
        Not by celebrity, money, sex,
    Much less destiny's call.
Stagecraft has withdrawn the deus ex machina.
Only base reason serves this orchestrated arena.
Nor is there tragedy for victims of a self-inflicted cosmos,
And the billions denied indifferent to what the storm meant,
Calamity and torment so flawlessly marketed
One might conclude that the embalmers' art
Began with a simian climb up the top 40 charts.
All of these imperialist spectacles:
        The old arts precisely because
They sound the abyss
From the Hollywood lips of lecherous conjurings,
Have given way to a prepubescent Judas kiss.
What happened to the optics in a word?
    This night there are sirens and sirens,
        Love and love's ruin;
        Beauty and beauty's ruin;
Desire and the terminus of desire.
Still and still in the moment
        Though contorted with sentiment,
Not yet all currency's consequence.
But let's not muddy this with hope.
The optics of the word have been converted to light
So that day belongs to darkest night. It belongs and,
 Has always been the fitting end
From which our senses reel;
Recoil from an embrace
        From scaly chimeras out of time and place.
Let there be tragedy.
Don't spin destiny, or falsify fate,
Even as the falsified cry out their writhings,
    Suffering purchase and
        Documented in funereal entertainments
    Long black snaking processions
And mourners momentarily startled genuine by their mistakes.

Mourners who murdered those by making them
        More than they are;
    Those that love them
So that they can more love themselves;
That credit them so that
They can more credit themselves.
Praise them so that they may praise themselves;
        So that all who buy profit from
What the corporate mind falsifies.
Who of us has not dashed up and down the stupid
            On the radio dial
Only to fall back on Beethoven or Bird?
Their magnanimity. Asking nothing.
Giving everything. Few of these flourish now
Strangled in the green overgrowth
And in the sugars that runnel our veins.
        Few pains needed to deny them
    Be it by their junk or junk or junk;
    White skin or white powder
Over the rust of nescience.
Those artists that tipped us off to the end of tragedy,
        Dadaists, Beats and bank tellers.
That in Bruno's cosmos
You cannot make your own mistakes.
        You are never master of your own fate
Be it a nephew or the needle.
No matter how the performers are overdubbed to sound,
    Scrubbed to look like cowboys and hipsters,
Nazis and common thugs;
The joke endures as long as the bottom line
Remains the punch line,
No matter how many in so many ways
            Thought they were saying that,
Stumbling over their exemplars.
Is it because we are corporeal opposites of our creations
        That we embrace Mammon's tyranny;
Open the screen door to the grinning salesman
As he tips his Hamburg;

Turn on the radio
    And buy the jingo. Buy back a portion of ourselves.
        What's left?
    We buy back what we already think we are,
Sweetened at the end of a needle or optical laser.
Who does that? Buys back their being?
What visionary would chase such tales?
All this mock revolution going in circles,
Dizzy trying to read the label on the turntable;
    With our purchase power and our severed heads
And devalue lest we extinguish the phantast;
Or the mechanical replication of visions aural cousin
        That of its own hears no voices
Yet by fixed component makes the choices.
Who hears the Ancient Voices of Children?
      Far too few to challenge money's quorum.
  Or 'The Jupiter' that like the planet
        Makes world's possible?
Who sings 'Diesen Kuss der ganzen Welt?'
 Instead death is all about this room,
Tuning, tuning, tuning to twin holocausts.
Sediment settles in the ashtray of the stars.
An ascension to the bottom by all of the top dogs.
Rock hardens in the Grand Inversion.
A world that stands on its head for my amusement.
Hah!

111

About the author

Carlo Parcelli studied and worked for many years with the Joyce/Wake scholar, Dr. Rudd Fleming, who translated Greek drama with Ezra Pound while Pound was incarcerated at St. Elizabeth's Hospital in Washington, DC. He has published two books in the style of Pound's Cantos, 'Three Antiphonies' and 'Fernparallelismus'.

He has also published a series of 88 monologues, 'The Gospel According to Simon Kananaios: A Meditation on Empire' based on the Anglo/Welsh poet David Jones' monologues of a Roman principalis in his volume 'The Sleeping Lord'. Carlo has a forthcoming epic poem about a fictitious First Century Roman cynic philosopher called 'Canus Ictus in Exilium' (Dog Bite in Exile). His work, generally excerpted, has appeared in a number of journals including Exquisite Corpse, Make It New, Brave New Word and Science as Culture. He has performed his work, especially 'The Gospel' at dozens of venues including the Boog Poetry Festival, The National Beat Poetry Festival, The Bowery Poetry Club and Busboys and Poets in Washington, DC. He is currently an editor at Flashpoint magazine:

http://www.flashpointmag.com/, an online journal largely devoted to high-Modernist poetics.

www.ingramcontent.com/pod-product-compliance
Lightning Source LLC
Chambersburg PA
CBHW021306090726
47818CB00086B/310/J